MW01041779

West Chester History

A Review in Early Postcards

Monument to the 97th R. V.
West Chester, Pa.

STATE NORMAL SCHOOL WEST CHESTER

THE STUDENT BAND: STATE NORMAL SCHOOL, WEST CHESTER, PA.

ENTRANCE PHILIP'S MEMORIAL CHAPEL
STATE TEACHERS COLLEGE WEST CHESTER PA

Schiffer Publishing Ltd

William Schultz
& Robert Sheller

4880 Lower Valley Road   Atglen, Pennsylvania 19310

Dedication

This book is dedicated to:

Jake William Schultz, born September 6, 2006, first grandchild.

• • • • •

Christian Michael Gatlos, born October 29, 2000, first grandchild

• • • • •

Michael R.J Micciche, born June 30, 2003, second grandchild

• • • • •

All the West Chester postcard collectors and historians

Acknowledgments

The authors would like to express their appreciation to the following for their support and encouragement in the completing of this book:

- Of course, the late and beloved historian Paul A. Rodebaugh.
- The Sheller Family ((Stephanie, Valerie, Kristin and Joshua)
- The Schultz Family (Patricia, Derek, & Sherri)
- Mr. David Rhoades
- Ms. Donna White
- Mr. Harvy Fingerhood
- Mr. Jim Jones

Published by Schiffer Publishing Ltd.
4880 Lower Valley Road
Atglen, PA 19310
Phone: (610) 593-1777; Fax: (610) 593-2002
E-mail: Info@schifferbooks.com

For the largest selection of fine reference books on this and related subjects, please visit our web site at
www.schifferbooks.com
We are always looking for people to write books on new and related subjects. If you have an idea for a book please contact us at the above address.

This book may be purchased from the publisher.
Include $3.95 for shipping.
Please try your bookstore first.
You may write for a free catalog.

In Europe, Schiffer books are distributed by
Bushwood Books
6 Marksbury Ave.
Kew Gardens
Surrey TW9 4JF England
Phone: 44 (0) 20 8392-8585; Fax: 44 (0) 20 8392-9876
E-mail: info@bushwoodbooks.co.uk
Website: www.bushwoodbooks.co.uk
Free postage in the U.K., Europe; air mail at cost.

Copyright © 2007 by William Schultz and Robert Sheller
Library of Congress Control Number: 2007928797

All rights reserved. No part of this work may be reproduced or used in any form or by any means—graphic, electronic, or mechanical, including photocopying or information storage and retrieval systems—without written permission from the publisher.

The scanning, uploading and distribution of this book or any part thereof via the Internet or via any other means without the permission of the publisher is illegal and punishable by law. Please purchase only authorized editions and do not participate in or encourage the electronic piracy of copyrighted materials.

"Schiffer," "Schiffer Publishing Ltd. & Design," and the "Design of pen and ink well" are registered trademarks of Schiffer Publishing Ltd.

Designed by Mark David Bowyer
Type set in Arrus BT / Korinna BT

ISBN: 978-0-7643-2707-0
Printed in China

Contents

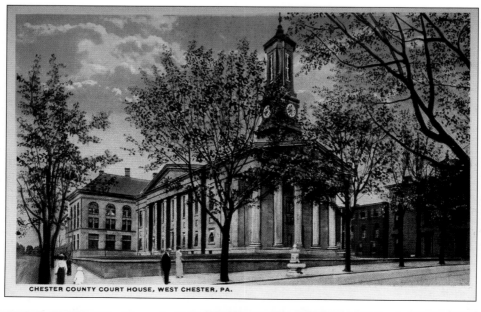

CHESTER COUNTY COURT HOUSE, WEST CHESTER, PA.

Introduction

In 1999 the Borough of West Chester, Pennsylvania, celebrated its 200th anniversary of its founding. Those of us who have lived in the community fondly remember these past images of our developing borough. They are pictures of townsfolk, celebrations, buildings or other events that have touched upon our memories. Even though time has changed the landscape and building facades, many of the original structures remain to this day. Almost everyone in the community knows Benny's Pizzeria located on North Church Street, West Chester. Before there was Benny's, there was a business known as Johnny and Connie's Market.

By examining old West Chester postcards, we step through the portals of time and witness the development of our town. With the contributions of avid collectors and use of our own collections, we have arranged a collage of images and recorded events to capture a fleeting time in the evolution of our community. Occasionally the postcards are similar, giving differing perspectives on the same scene. We believe that some of the unique postcards have never been published in earlier books. We are excited that many of the postcards in this book have are rare and seldom seen.

As each chapter unfolds, you will see a community's evolution and progress captured through the lens of the photographer's camera. Although many of the depicted scenes are now just memories of a distant past, we sincerely hope that our presentation takes our reader back to an earlier time. For some it may awaken in them fond recollections of their experiences back then. For others they may gain a new appreciation of the growth of the community and the contributions of those who have gone before.

For the Collector: A Pricing Guide to West Chester, PA Postcards [As of June 30, 2007]

Deltiology, the formal name for postcard collecting, is considered to be one of the top three collection hobbies of the world. As early as 1861, a postcard copyright was issued to John P. Charlton of Philadelphia, Pennsylvania. Eventually that copyright was transferred to H.L. Lipman. Until 1873, the Lipman Postal Cards were sold to the general public. They were gradually replaced by U.S. Government Postal Cards.

To assist deltiologists, the authors have selected 4 price levels for the cards in this book and include the codes with each caption. These evaluations are based on their combined years of experience in buying/selling/collecting postcards.

(A) Postcard in very fine unused condition should be available under $5.00

(B) Postcard in very fine unused condition should be available from $5.01 to $ 9.99

(C) Postcard in very fine unused condition should be available from $10.00 to $25.00

(D) Postcard in very fine unused condition should be available from $25.01 to $100.00+

Note: Some West Chester postcards in the marketplace will exceed $100.00

The prices above should be adjusted for condition, scarcity, postmarks, and other interesting additions/deletions/errors and of course the difficulty of acquisition.

Postcard Publishers Referenced in this Book,

ACMEGRAPH: The Acmegraph Co., Chicago, Ill.
ALBERTYPE: The Albertype Co., Brooklyn, NY
AMERICAN ART POST CARD CO.: C.T. American Art, Chicago
AMERICAN NEWS CO.: American News Company, New York, Leipzig, Berlin, Dresden
AMERICAN POST CARD CO.: American Post Card Co., Lancaster, PA
ARTVUE POSTCARD CO.: Artvue Post Card Co., New York, NY
BEAU ART: Beau Art Photo Co., Trenton, NJ
BELT: J. W. Belt, Photographer, West Chester, PA

BOYER: Lynn H. Boyer Jr., Wildwood, NJ
C.T. AMERICAN ART: C.T. American Art, Chicago
CRAVEN: Craven & Co,, Doylestown, PA
CURT TEICH AND CO.: Curt Teich & Co., Chicago
DAWSON: E. J. Dawson, West Chester
DEHAVEN: H. V. Dehaven, West Chester
EAGLE: Eagle Post card Company, New York City
FATH, P. F. Fath, West Chester
GOODE: Goode Photography, Frazier, PA
GRAYCRAFT: Graycraft Card Co., Danville, VA
HENRY: A. Henry, West Chester
KIRBY: F. M. Kirby Co.
KROPP: E. C. Kropp Co., Milwaukee, WI
MERRILL: Haydon Ord Merrill, Upper Darby, PA
MERRIMACK: Merrimack Post card, West Suffield, CT
MILLER: Ruth & Hugh Miller Jr., Philadelphia, PA
MOORE: Philip H. Moore, Media, PA.
PAINE: Brian Payne, Photographer, Houston, TX
PARKER: S. J. Parker and Son, West Chester
PHOTOGRAVURE: Photogravure Post Card Co., Philadelphia
PHOTOSTINT: Photostint, Detroit, MI
PIERCE: W. A. Pierce, West Chester
PMC: Private Mailing Card
POSTCARD DIST. CO.: Post Card Distributing Co., Philadelphia
ROCHELLE: Fred W. Rochelle, Philadelphia
ROTOGRAPH: The Rotograph Co., New York City
RUBEN: Ruben Photograph Cards, Newburgh, NY
TICHNOR BROTHERS: Tichnor Brothers, Boston, MA
TUCK: Raphel Tuck and Son, London, Paris, New York, West Chester
VURE: Vure Post card Co., Philadelphia
WYCO: Wyco Products, Jenkintown, PA

The Farmers' Hotel — West Chester, Pa.

CHAPTER 1

The Main Streets

Gay, Market, Chestnut, Church, Virginia, High, Marshall, and Matlack, are a few of the familiar boulevard names in the historic town of West Chester. The streets played a major role in the progress of the borough and in distant times delineated the boundary lines of the early property owners.

In 1829 and 1830, Gay and Church Streets in West Chester were paved for the first time, long after a road from Wilmington, Delaware, to Reading, in Berks County, via West Chester was built. It was extended in 1803 with a turnpike from Downington to Harrisburg via Honeybrook and Ephrata, and became well known as the "Horseshoe Pike." Since West Chester was originally a crossroads village the first chapter fittingly focuses on the streets of West Chester.

Miner, Nields, Darlington, Barnard, Price, Rosedale, Franklin, Biddle, Walnut, Washington, Ashbridge, Maple, Adams, Lafayette, Sharpless, New, Magnolia, Union, Everhart, Linden, Lacey, Goshen, Dean, College, Penn, Montgomery, Bolmar, Patton, Bradford, and Wayne; the enchanted names of West Chester streets reflect their charm and interest. They are wonderful places to stroll and view the municipality, giving you a chance to experience with your own senses the places, and, to some extent, the times viewed in these postcards.

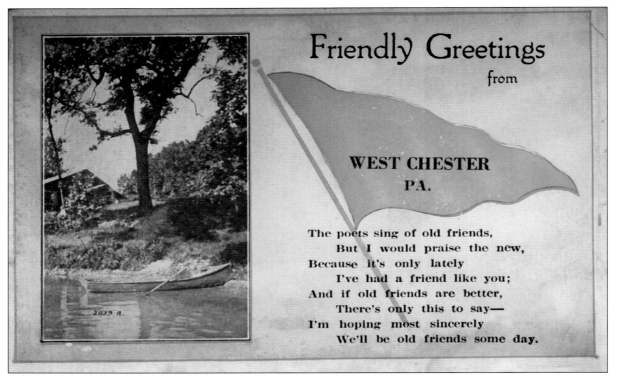

Early greeting postcard. West Chester is located on a ridge of land 450 feet above sea level between the Chester and Brandywine Creeks, about 24 miles west of Philadelphia. Native Americans had favored the region, as evidenced by nine campsites found within the present borough discovered by Alfred Sharples in the 1880s. The Great Minquas Trail used by Native Americans as an important trade route west to the Susquehanna passed through this area. (C)

Birds-eye view of West Chester, Pa.

Birds-eye view postcard. One of the three original counties of Pennsylvania formed by William Penn in November 1682. It did not become an inland county until 1789. Its name derives from Cheshire (i.e., Chester-shire), England, from which many of its early settlers came. West Chester, the county seat since 1788, was incorporated as a borough on March 28, 1799. It was named for Chester, the older county seat (now in Delaware County), which in turn derived its name from the shire town of Cheshire. (B)

West Chester, Pa.

West Market Street.

No. 3751a

Patented Dec. 5th, 1905. No. 806631.

Postcard with foldout showing other scenes of West Chester. A fairly scarce West Market Street view. The Rotograph Co. postcard with the clip holding the foldout intact. (D)

West Market Street and Fountain, West Chester, Pa.

The Everhart Fountain donated by John Roskell Everhart. The West Chester Downtown Historic District includes approximately 15 square blocks of the Borough. Central to this area are five blocks along the Borough's two parallel "Main Streets," Gay and Market. This area includes the original town plot (1784 — the four blocks bordering Gay and High Streets) and subsequent commercial expansion to the east and west along Gay and Market Streets. A Rotograph Co. postcard. (A)

WEST MARKET STREET, WEST CHESTER, PA.

West Market Street, unpaved, c.1908, shown on a Rotograph Co. postcard.
In 1907, the U.S. Post Office began to allow one to write on the back left side, hence the name "divided back" postcards. Postcard collections provide unique and engaging images of life in early twentieth century America. In the decades following 1900, people bought, sent, and collected postcards in staggering numbers. (A)

West Gay Street view, c. 1905; note pavement. A Parker & Sons postcard.
The United States Post Office Department issued America's first postal card on May 13, 1873.
The indicia on the buff-colored card depicted the bust of Liberty and the inscription
"U S Postage - One Cent" in an oval. (C)

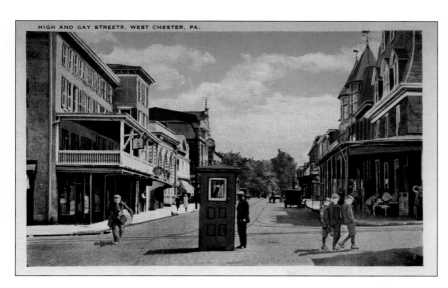

High and Gay Streets, a Fath
Postcard, with a view of the traffic
coordinator. During the summer
months, the booth was replaced
with a hand-turned traffic sign.

Seldom seen, Kirby-published
postcard view of Gay and
Church Streets.
Postcard collecting provides
unique and engaging images
of life in the early twentieth
century America. (C)

A fairly scarce view on this Parker & Sons published postcard, depicts the area around the crossing of the Wilmington and Philadelphia Roads (present-day High and Gay Streets, respectively). This remained farmland until 1760, when a log schoolhouse was erected at the northwest corner of the intersection. High Street was named for the fact it ran along the elevated area between the Brandywine Creek and the Chester Creek. (B)

Strolling along High Street in 1908. Postcard published by Rotograph.
The postcard fad was fed by a confluence of several factors: the development of photography, new printing and publishing technology, a heightened interest in travel, cheap postal rates, and perhaps most important, time for hobbies, which included collecting. (A)

South High Street view on a seldom seen oval postcard. Oval cards are very desirable to deltiologists. This is a Parker & Sons postcard. Samuel Parker's business was located in the heart of downtown West Chester. (C)

A Henry-published view of South High Street, c.1908. High Street remains a key north-south avenue through the Borough. Car barn door of the street railway is on the right side. In 1898 the U.S. Government authorized private postcards, the forerunners of the picture view postcards. (A)

S. J. Parker & Sons oval postcard showing North Church Street, c.1906 (C)

NORTH CHURCH ST., WEST CHESTER, PA

A view of A. Henry storefront in the 50 block of N. Church Street in 1906. A. Henry was a significant postcard publisher in West Chester. This postcard is seldom found in postcard collections of West Chester. (C)

Church Street looking north, c.1905. *The use of the word "POST CARD/POSTCARD" (as one or two words) was granted by the government to private printers on Dec. 24, 1901. Writing was still not permitted on the address side. The publishing of printed postcards during this time doubled almost every six months.* (D)

CHURCH ST., WEST CHESTER, PA.

CHURCH STREET FROM EAST GAY STREET BY MOONLIGHT, WEST CHESTER, Pa.

A. Henry published postcard showing Church Street at night. Today, Church Street is an important venue for businesses and retail outlets in West Chester. *In America, postcard collecting is sometimes known as Deltiology, a modern word coined from the ancient Greek for a writing tablet, and collectors may be referred to as deltiologists. Although "postcarditis" is not the fad it was a hundred years ago, it is still claimed to be the third largest collecting hobby after philately and coin collecting.* (A)

Beautiful and scenic unpaved Rosedale Avenue that borders the campus of the West Chester University on the south side of the borough as seen c.1914. This is a Parker & Sons postcard. (B)

A Parker & Sons-published postcard reflecting the rural nature of the town as late as 1906. This view is of West Miner Street. The building on the left is Old Zion Church. (B)

The tranquil beauty of West Union Street, c.1915, in the Borough. Postcard Dist. Co.-published postcard. (A)

CHAPTER 2

The Architecture
The "Athens of Pennsylvania"

Ah, the architecture of West Chester!

People from all over travel to West Chester to see the old buildings and the classic examples of architecture that line the streets of this Pennsylvania county seat. These postcards try to capture the architectural splendor of this town.

The National Trust for Historic Preservation has described the borough as follows:

> "Although West Chester, Pennsylvania, a former Quaker town incorporated in 1799, is only 1.8 square miles, it's teeming with 19th-century charm. Nearly 90 percent of the picture-perfect borough — with its lovely town center and famed brick sidewalks — is listed in the National Register of Historic Places. Located in the heart of the Brandywine Valley near three Pennsylvania Revolutionary War historic sites — Brandywine, Paoli, and Valley Forge — West Chester today is a university and residential community with fine examples of Victorian and Greek Revival architecture, including the Chester County Courthouse, designed by Thomas U. Walter, one of the architects of the U.S. Capitol. The borough's small size means that West Chester is a 'walkable' community, home to dozens of outstanding restaurants, art galleries and retail shops.

> "'West Chester is an historic destination that has achieved a standard many communities strive to emulate,' said Richard Moe, president of the National Trust for Historic Preservation. 'West Chester is a real, living, dynamic town that appreciates and capitalizes on its rich past, while keeping a watchful eye on the future.'" *(http://www.nationaltrust.org/dozen_distinctive_destinations/westchester.html)*

For these reasons, the National Trust for Historic Preservation, the country's largest private, nonprofit preservation organization, named West Chester, Pennsylvania, to its 2006 list of America's Dozen Distinctive Destinations, an annual list of unique and lovingly preserved communities in the United States. Individuals, preservation organizations and local communities selected it from 93 destinations in 39 states that were nominated.

Chester County Prison. Built in 1838 at the corner of Market and New Streets, it remained in operation until a new prison was built in 1959 (*Daily Local News*, May 5, 1955). It was designed to hold approximately 100 inmates. In 1900, the facility was a family-run institution. This is a c.1908 view by Parker and Sons. Building was demolished in the 1950s. (C)

The West Chester Library. Located at 415 N. Church St. at Lafayette Street on the north side. The library has recently been renovated, but maintained the original façade and structure appropriately. Founded by a small group of civic-minded West Chester residents in 1872, the library was housed at various West Chester addresses until 1888, when the present building was dedicated and opened to the public. A fine Parker & Sons postcard. (B)

The Municipal Building is located at 15 South High Street and now houses a restaurant. The Borough was incorporated in 1799 and moved into this building in 1912. A Diamond W published postcard c.1913. (D)

The Barclay Home, West Chester, Pa. *This is where Mrs. G. lives now. Edith*

Also known as the Joshua Hartshorne Estate in North Hills at 535 and 539 N. Church Street, it is Italianate and Colonial Revival in style. The building is on the National Historic Register listing. A Parker and Sons postcard. (B)

The Armory, West Chester, Pa.

A Parker & Sons postcard showing the Armory (originally a church) located on West Gay Street. The building has been demolished. (C)

ELKS BUILDING, WEST CHESTER, PA.

The Elks Building. West Chester Lodge #853 was chartered in 1903 and has been serving the community for over 100 years. The entire downtown district is listed on the National Register of Historic Places. This historic building is located on North High Street. A Rotograph Co. postcard postmarked 1916. (A)

Samuel Parker and Sons, located at 18 W. Gay Street, noted publisher of postcards. This postcard is a very fine example of a difficult postcard to locate. Parker and Sons was the most prolific publisher of West Chester postcards exceeding 300 different cards of the area. (D)

S. J. Parker and Son, 19 West Gay st., West Chester, Pa.
(Established 1859 by Saml. J. Parker)

MEMORIAL HALL, WEST CHESTER, PA.
Home of Gen. Geo. A. McCall Post, No. 31, G. A. R.

October 1907.

Memorial Hall, dated 1907. Memorial Hall was built in 1848 and today houses part of the Chester County Historical Society on N. High Street just above Chestnut Street. (C)

Established 1853   Incorporated 1907

Philadelphia Office   Over 600 Acres in
Stephen Girard Building   Nurseries

Office of Hoopes, Bro. & Thomas Company
West Chester. Pa.

Hoopes Brothers and Thomas was established in 1855 and sold nearly 900,000 seedlings of various fruit trees yearly in the 1890s. Oval postcard; publisher unknown at this time. (B)

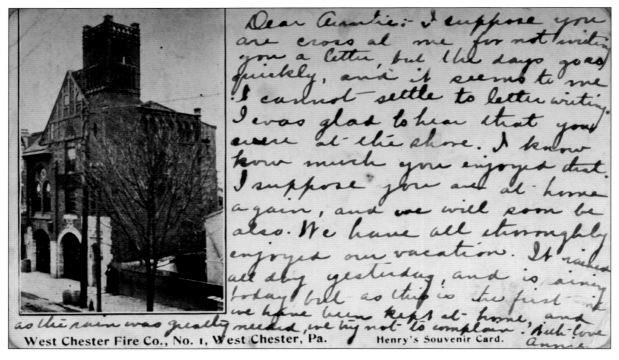

West Chester Fire Co., No. 1, West Chester, Pa.   Henry's Souvenir Card.

An example, in the Historic District, of Queen Anne style architecture is the First West Chester Fire Company at 14 North Church Street. Splendid Queen Anne examples are found along North Church Street. This is a Henry postcard postmarked 1905. (D)

Good Will Fire Co., No. 2, West Chester, Pa.

Henry's Souvenir Card.

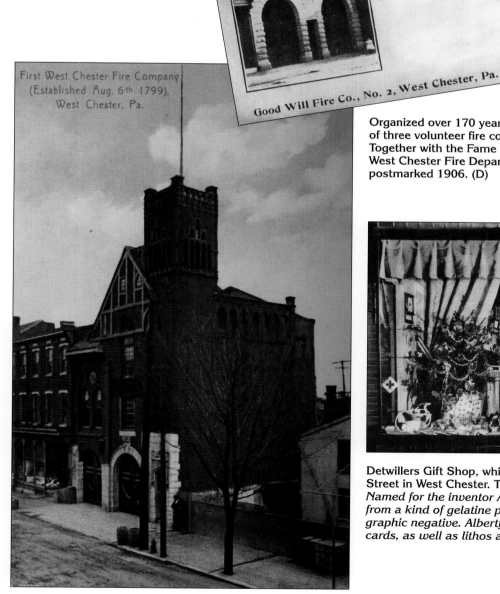

First West Chester Fire Company (Established Aug. 6th 1799), West Chester, Pa.

Organized over 170 years ago in 1833, the Good Will is one of three volunteer fire companies that serve the community. Together with the Fame Fire Co., three stations make up the West Chester Fire Department. This is an Henry postcard postmarked 1906. (D)

Detwillers Gift Shop, which was located at 34 South High Street in West Chester. This Albertype-published postcard. *Named for the inventor Albert of Munich, thea picture printed from a kind of gelatine plate produced by means of a photographic negative. Albertype produced handcolored postcards, as well as lithos and other styles.* (C)

First West Chester Fire Co., est. 1799, shown on this Parker and Sons card. The West Chester Fire Company was the first fire company in West Chester. The "Wessies" are now located at Miner Street and Bradford Avenue. (D)

The Art Center on North Church Street. A DeHaven-published postcard.
Dating: Many vintage postcards such as the Detroit Publishing Company (aka known as Detroit Photographic) put copyright dates right on the card (about 1898-1907). These dates usually applied to the image and in many cases the postcard was actually printed a few years later. This card bears a 1940 postmark. (D)

The Hickman Memorial Hall. A WYCO postcard. *Used or Unused: Vintage postcards with writing (and stamps and cancels) are actually sometimes just as valuable as those that have no marks. There is genealogical interest in what is written and some times historical or biographical value as well.* (A)

Town's End. Built in 1908 at E. Chestnut and N. High Streets. A Belt postcard view. *The size of the town pricing factor: Generally speaking the smaller the town such as West Chester, the more valuable the vintage postcard, but there are so many exceptions that is hard to make to make a firm statement.* (C)

The Shipley home located on Hillendale Road shown on this Parker and Sons postcard. A 1910 postmark on the reverse. (A)

Located on South High Street (at Lacey St.) this view of the New Century Club was published by Tichnor.Bros., Inc. Women formed the Club in 1893. The building pictured was completed in 1915 having been designed by R. E. White of Philadelphia in a Colonial style. (C)

The Post Office. Construction began c.1905 on the large Post Office located on E. Gay Street. The first West Chester P. O. opened September 7, 1802 with Mr. Cromwell Pierce the first Postmaster. Parker and Sons postcard. (A)

MANSION HOUSE, WEST CHESTER, PA.   JAMES C. MILLHIZER, PROP.

Mansion House Hotel, located at the corner of Church and Market Streets, was designed by William Strickland, the architect of the famous Second Bank in Philadelphia. Strickland was the first of a series of celebrated architects to work in West Chester. Thomas U. Walter was a Strickland's protégé. Unusual postcard by C. T. American as the proprietor is named on the face. (C)

A Fath postcard depicting the lovely West Chester Country Club located at Ashbridge and N. High Streets. Built in 1907 this clubhouse was replaced after a fire destroyed it. *Postcards were the rage between 1901- 1914. Millions were sold but have you ever wondered why? Because this was before the masses were exposed to television, radio, and the horseless carriage (the auto). For example, folks from Iowa may have gotten their only opportunity to see West Chester, Pennsylvania by trading post-cards with relatives or "penpals."* (B)

Johnny and Connie's Market at 100 N. Church Street shown in 1950. Today Benny's Pizza Parlor utilizes the building. (D)

CHAPTER 3

The Town Folks

The citizens of West Chester generally are not highlighted on the historical postcards with some exceptions. Many of the postcards shown in this chapter are the non-famous people-related vintage examples.

Brinton, Pennypacker, Darlington, Barnard, Miner, Biddle, Sharples(s), Matlack, Hickman, Everhart, Pyle, Barber, Lewis, Bell, Everhart, Butler, Painter, Hoopes, Hannum, Taylor, May, Rothrock, Hayes, Futhey, Cope, MacElree, Marshall, Philips, Townsend, Worthington and Haines are names that just roll off the tongue of the historians of West Chester.

But there are also names of modern figures in West Chester history for future historians to remember and write about someday: Zukin, Sheller, Hagerty, Dinniman, Schauer, Rodebaugh, DeBaptiste, Ott, Gavin, Mowday, Yoder, Winters, Gilmore, Swope, Featherman, Enoches, Wilson, Jones, Brown, Patton, Cairns, Wood, Wing-Adler, Wingard, Van Grofski, Mauger, Patton, Naylor, McCarthy, Loftus, Knox, Quinn, Warner, and Graver.

A Favorite Son

In any pantheon of American musicians, Samuel Barber, commands a prominent niche. Along with the works of Aaron Copland and George Gershwin, his compositions are in the repertoire of the world's finest musicians. He has become almost popular — a word that would make him cringe. Barber would be amused and amazed by all this, for he often called himself "a living dead" American composer.

Certainly in the early years he was in many ways the spoiled darling of the gods. He was born into a comfortable, educated, social, and distinguished American family (he was related to Robert Fulton) in West Chester, Pennsylvania on 9th of March 1910. He was spared the virtues of poverty and never enjoyed the values of starving in a garret. His father was a doctor, an Episcopalian pillar of society, his mother was a sensitive amateur pianist. His aunt, Louise Homer, a leading soprano at the Metropolitan Opera, was married to Sidney Homer, a respectable composer of American art songs. Perhaps more than anybody it was Homer who molded the integrity and aesthetic values of his nephew. When he died in 1953 Barber was profoundly grieved.—G. Shirmer Inc. **[[[Was this a quotation from G. Shirmer, Inc.? If so I'll need to go back and un-edit it and you will need to provide a more complete citation.]]]**

Guess who's here
in West Chester, Pa.

The borough celebrated its one-hundredth birthday in 1899 and the population had grown to nearly 9,500, the largest municipality in Chester County, with nearly ten percent of the county's residents living in the borough. This is a c.1905 postcard by #861. *Until the middle of the 19th century, people mailed messages to each other via the privacy of sealed letters. The idea for the postal card originated in Germany in 1865. However, the Austrian government issued the first postal card. The early postal cards had their detractors. Many people thought it improper to mail messages on cards that anyone, especially the servants, could read.* (C)

266
BURGESS PENNYPACKER
OF WEST CHESTER, PA.

Charles H. Pennypacker a prominent lawyer, amateur scientist, active politician, born in 1845. This is a Rotograph Co. postcard. Mr. Pennypacker became the Burgess (Mayor) of West Chester. This postcard is postmarked 1906. *A popular publisher was The Rotograph Postcard Company located in New York City and Chicago. This company published a variety of subjects ranging from scenic views of towns and cities to real photos.* (C)

The Marshall Residence, real photo type postcard dated 1908. This is a relatively scarce Craven published postcard. This is the home of Anne Y. Stone located on the corner of Market and Walnut Sts. Ms. Stone was the last surviving charter member of the Westminster Presbyterian Church. The Salvation Army is now located on this corner. (D)

10-5-08

H. M. Stone.

Real photo type postcard showing many West Chester residents. (B)

Virginia Avenue. Parker and Sons postcard, c.1906.
In 1901, the U.S. Government granted the use of the words "Post Card" to be printed on the undivided back of privately printed cards and allowed publishers to drop the authorization inscription previously required. As in earlier eras, writing was still limited to the front. However, during this time, other countries began to permit the use of a divided back. This enabled the front to be used exclusively for the design, while the back was divided so that the left side was for writing messages and the right side for the address. England was the first to permit the divided back in 1902, France followed in 1904, Germany in 1905 and finally the U.S. in 1907. These changes ushered in the "Golden Age" of postcards as millions were sold and used. (B)

Founder's Week Parade in Philadelphia, 1908, showing West Chester's Fame Fire Company (#3) marching. A William Ray postcard. (D)

Play Grounds, Darlington Seminary. A Hermann postcard, c.1906. (C)

The West Chester Hunt. Parker and Sons postcard c.1907. (A)

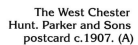

The West Chester Post Office. A Kirby Co. postcard c.1910.
The United States Post Office Department issued America's first postal card on May 13, 1873. (A)

Real photo type postcard showing the Marine Band at the celebration of the unveiling of Old Glory in front of the Courthouse on June 11, 1915, dating this seldom seen card. Sharples Park was located at the corner of Gay and Penn Streets. (D)

Women strolling on one of the beautiful streets of West Chester.
A colorful 1908 postmarked Rotograph Co. card. (A)

View of J. Warren Frame Grocery Store. A Craven published real photo type postcard postally cancelled in 1910. Frame's grocery store was located at 118 E. Market St, just east of M.S. Yearsleys building. (*Images of America, West Chester,* Martha Carson-Gentry and Paul Rodebaugh 1997) (D)

Parker and Sons postcard (1909 postmark) showing the RFD Carrier on the Paoli Road. In October 1896, Congress approved the establishment of rural free delivery of the mail. (C)

Early view of the center of West Chester on this postally used card from 1905. (D)

HIGH AND GAY STREETS, WEST CHESTER, PA.

Rotograph Co. postcard highlighting the business section, c.1906. (A)

A 3747 West Market Street, West Chester, Pa.

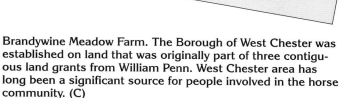

Brandywine Meadow Farm. The Borough of West Chester was established on land that was originally part of three contiguous land grants from William Penn. West Chester area has long been a significant source for people involved in the horse community. (C)

Chester County Trust Company shown on classic Parker and Sons postcard. The Great Depression caused the demise of the Sharples Separator Company, The Chester County Trust Company, and the Farmers and Mechanics Bank. (B)

A view showing the busy intersection. A Henry Co. postcard. Note the different forms of transportation. In 1901 there were only 175 telephones in the Borough.

A popular publisher in the early 1900s was The Albertype Company of Brooklyn, NY. Herman L. Wittemann owned the company and he published postcards from 1890 to 1952. Wittemann used a photo process invented by Austrian photographer Joseph Albert (1825-1886). His postcards used a special process. Wittemann's representatives would take photographs and he also would arrange to use photographs taken by others. (B)

CHAPTER 4
Modes of Transportation

From horses, canoes, buggies, and wagons, through trolleys, buses, autos, and trains, to planes and helicopters, West Chester has a long history interwoven by the progress of transportation modalities in Chester County and beyond. Because of West Chester's location, the linkages with rail lines and trolley lines sprouted prior to the turn of the century in 1900.

The postcards shown in this chapter reflect the numerous modes and certainly highlight the era of the trolley in this historical county seat in southeastern Pennsylvania.

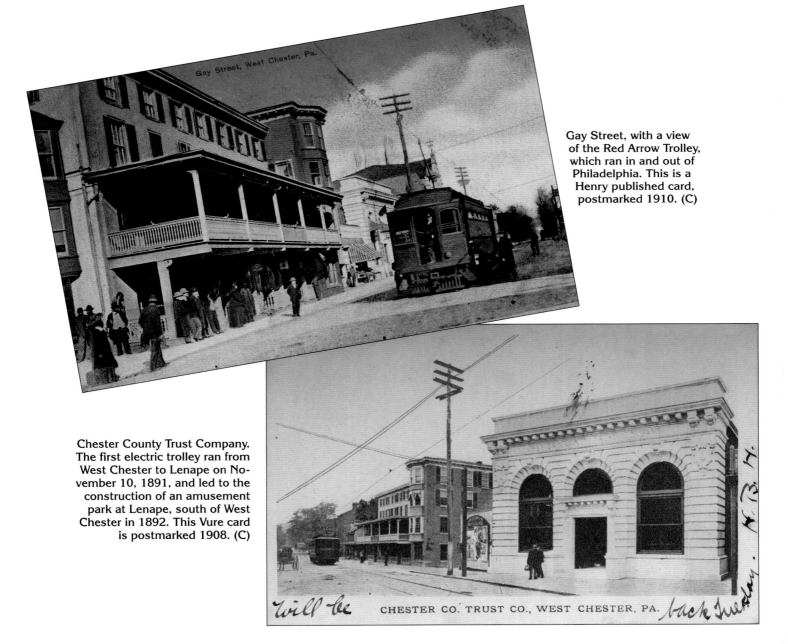

Gay Street, with a view of the Red Arrow Trolley, which ran in and out of Philadelphia. This is a Henry published card, postmarked 1910. (C)

Chester County Trust Company. The first electric trolley ran from West Chester to Lenape on November 10, 1891, and led to the construction of an amusement park at Lenape, south of West Chester in 1892. This Vure card is postmarked 1908. (C)

CHESTER CO. TRUST CO., WEST CHESTER, PA.

Green Tree Inn, West Chester, Pa.

Green Tree Inn. The growth of the trolley was amazing and by 1900 there were over 30,000 cars running over more than 15,000 miles of track in the U.S. The early cars were often the horse cars converted to electric cars but as time went on the size of the cars grew, as did the varieties of cars. 1908 postmark on the reverse of this American News Company card. (A)

Green Tree Inn, Corner High and Gay Streets, West Chester, Pa.

Green Tree Inn. Trolley companies created connections to Philadelphia by 1899, Downingtown by 1902, and Coatesville and Kennett Square by 1904. West Chester's favorite trolley was the "High Street Dinky," which provided local service between the State Normal School and the main trolley depot on Gay Street. This is an American News Co. card. (B)

Parker and Sons postcard showing a West Chester Street railway car in front of the Green Tree Hotel. (C)

1910 dated card showing the West Chester, Downingtown and Coatesville trolley on Market Street. (A)

1921 dated trolley by the Mansion House on colorful A. Henry view card. (B)

Gay Street, looking East from High Street,
West Chester, Pa.

A view of a Double-truck trolley car on Gay Street. 1915 postmark on this
C.T. Photochrome card. (C)

TURKS HEAD INN, WEST CHESTER, PA

Vehicles parked in front of the Turks Head Inn c.1935 (C)

An evening view of the Lenape trolley on Market Street. An A. Henry postcard. (A)

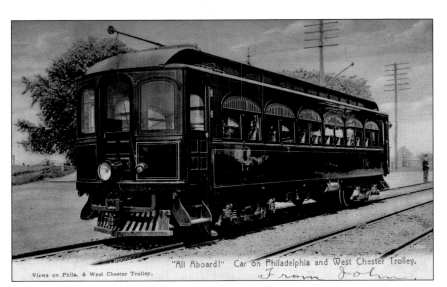

1907...All Aboard! In 1895, the Philadelphia and West Chester Traction Company was incorporated. In 1896 the trolley line was electrified and was completed between West Chester and Philadelphia in 1899. In 1936, the Philadelphia and West Chester Traction Co. was merged into the Philadelphia Suburban Transportation Company, which later became known as the Red Arrow Lines. Septa acquired the Philadelphia Suburban Train Company in 1970. A Moore postcard. (C)

Interior of a trolley car. A Moore postcard c.1907. (C)

P. R. R. Station, West Chester, Pa.

PRR Train Station, on a W. A. Pierce postcard postmarked 1919. Many believe this card is unique or exceptionally scarce. This is apt to be the most difficult to obtain postcard showing a scene from West Chester. The water tower in the background reads: 'West Chester Wheel Works, Hoopes Brothers and Darlington.' (Courtesy of the D. Rhoades Collection) (D)

PHILA. & WEST CHESTER TRACTION NO. 45
CENTER ENTRANCE STEEL INTERURBAN CAR - BUILT BY BRILL

In 1895, the Philadelphia & West Chester Traction Co. was incorporated, and acquired control of the Philadelphia & West Chester Turnpike Road Co., and the Philadelphia Castle Rock & West Chester Railway. In 1896 the line was electrified, and in 1899 was completed between Philadelphia and West Chester. (Railfan Exchange) (C)

The consolidation of streetcar and bus operations by the Philadelphia and West Chester Traction Company in the early 1930s gave rise to discussion of changing the corporate name to better reflect the new, diversified business. In 1936, the company became the Philadelphia Suburban Transportation Company, and adopted the "Red Arrow Lines" logo. (Paine postcard) (A)

Y. M. C. A., WEST CHESTER, PA.

Vehicle with folks out for drive past the Y.M.C.A. building. A Postcard Distributing Co. postcard.

Early Modern Era (White Border), 1916-1930 During this period, American technology advanced allowing printers to produce quality cards, although often they produced inferior ones in order to compete in the saturated market place. Public appeal changed and greeting card publication declined. However the view card market remained strong. The cards of this era were usually printed with white borders around the picture, thus the term "White Border Cards." (B)

Y. M. C. A., West Chester, Pa.

The Y.M,C,A on North High Street. A Kirby published card c.1912. (A)

Sales room of Franklin Autos shown on this Curt Teich & Co. card. The H. H. Franklin Manufacturing Company built the most successful American direct air-cooled cars from 1902 to 1934. The Company was run, during its first thirty-two years by Herbert H. Franklin, backer of the first die casting business. Cars in front of W. H. Wood. A nice advertisement postcard showing a late 20s Franklin and a 1905 vintage Franklin. (B)

1930 postmarked Fath postcard view of a nice look of a Ford Model T on this white border postcard of the Post Office on Gay Street.

The United States Post Office Department issued America's first postal card on May 13, 1873. The indicia on this buff-colored card depicts the bust of Liberty and the inscription "U S Postage - One Cent" in an oval. The card was issued on watermarked card stock. The watermark consists of the letters "U S P O D" in a 90mm x 60mm monogram. This watermark is found in the normal position, inverted, reversed, inverted, and reversed in combination. (B)

CHAPTER 5

The Banks

The West Chester Savings Bank was incorporated on March 6, 1900. The first officers of the bank were D.A. Boyer, President, and R.S. Warfel, Cashier, and the original directors of the bank were B.F. Tipton, J.B. Crayne, R.F. McFarlane, W.J. Mayer and E.H. Statler. On March 20, 1900, a construction contract was entered into with Frank Edgworthy to erect a two room, brick bank building in West Chester at a cost of $1,495. Additional costs incurred were $277.85 for the lot and $600.00 for the large vault. By June 23, 1900, the new building was ready for occupancy and a director's meeting was held. On July 16, 1900, the bank opened it doors for its initial day of business and the rest is history! *(Adapted from a statement of the West Chester Savings Bank)*

The First National Bank of West Chester opened its doors for business on January 2, 1864. The glass window in the banking room was inscribed: FIRST NATIONAL BANK.

The President of the Bank was George Brinton, but this was only a part time position. The bank initially opened at 19 N. High St. By the early 1900s, the Bank's continued growth made it imperative to find more adequate space. In May, 1911, the bank's board approved the purchase of the Hemphill Building located at 9 N. High St.

The First National Bank survives, but is now called the First National Bank of Chester County.

Postcards chronicle of the opening of one of the numerous banks in West Chester at the beginning of the Golden Age of Postcards **????**. Banks have always played a significant role in the history of West Chester and this chapter presents this postcard selection trying to capture the beauty and the impact of the banks of "old Turk's Head."

Chester County Trust Company on Gay Street. ATC Comp postcard postmarked 1911.
Divided Back Era of Postcards, 1907-1915 By this period, divided backs were almost universal, except in a few monopolistic governments. Previous to and during this period, a majority of U.S. postcards were printed in Europe, especially in Germany whose printing methods were regarded as the best in the world. However the trying years of this period, the rising import tariffs and the threats of war, caused a swift decline in the cards imported. Thus the political strains of the day brought about the end of the "Golden Age" of postcards. (C)

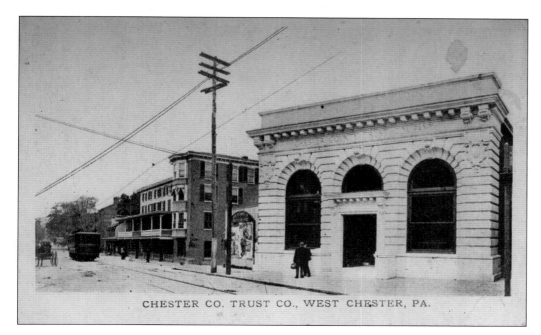

CHESTER CO. TRUST CO., WEST CHESTER, PA.

The 1905 Chester County Trust Company on East Gay Street, in the Historic District, is a small example of Beaux-Arts architecture, a style named after the Ecole des Beaux-Arts in Paris. The boldness of the rusticated joints, and the use of arches in conjunction with the classical orders, are among the characteristics of the style. Arches distinguish this Beaux-Arts building from Greek Revival. A Vure card. (C)

The First National Bank, West Chester, Pa.

In 1836, Thomas U. Walter designed the First National Bank of West Chester which opened its doors for business on January 2, 1864. The President of the Bank was George Brinton, but this was only a part time position. The bank initially opened at 19 N. High Street. The glass window in the banking room was inscribed: FIRST NATIONAL BANK. The Bank was across from the courthouse on High Street. He used the Doric order, and the building, despite an alteration to the steps so that they cut into the podium, is a supremely successful instance of Greek revival architecture. (The handsome bronze doors are set into another battered doorway.) This is an elusive Pierce published postcard. (B)

THE FIRST NATIONAL BANK, WEST CHESTER, PA.

Public edifices like churches and government buildings usage of the Greek Revival style is most impressive. The appeal of this classicism is evidenced by the Neoclassical Revival structure at the First National Bank and was remodeled in 1912 employing the Roman form of the Ionic order. The First National Bank is the only surviving bank from over 100 years ago, and is now called the First National Bank of Chester County. By the early 1900s, the Bank's continued growth made it imperative to find more adequate space. In May of 1911, the Bank Board approved the purchase of the Hemphill Building located at 9 N. High St. An American Art Post Card Co. view. (A)

FARMERS NATIONAL BANK BUILDING
TO BE ERECTED ON S W COR HIGH AND MARKET STREETS
WEST CHESTER, PA.

ABOVE PICTURE is from the architect's plans, for the new home of THE FARMERS NATIONAL BANK. The construction will be of stone, iron and cement —the best assurance of safety and security that modern architects know.

More commodious accommodations will be provided for the transaction of financial business than are now offered in Chester county.

The location is the most accessible and convenient in West Chester.

Trolley cars from west and north pass the doors; and the terminus of the Philadelphia line is but a block away.

Farmers and Merchants Building. This bank building was built in 1907 at Market and High Streets in the center of the Borough. This is a fairly scarce postcard. (C)

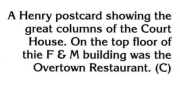

18795—Farmers & Mechanics Trust Co. Bldg., West Chester, Pa.

The Farmers and Merchants Building rose at the southwest corner of High and Market Streets. Its six stories on a steel skeleton make it, in principle, a true skyscraper. This is a Beaux-Arts design, with a clear differentiation of the podium or base story, the upward sweep of the four central stories with their oriel bays, and the triforium top story with emphatic cornice. (A)

The Greek Revival architecture along High Street that gives West Chester the nickname Athens of the West. Within the Borough limits, there are over 3,000 structures dating back to the colonial period. A Sexichrome card. (B)

A Henry postcard showing the great columns of the Court House. On the top floor of thie F & M building was the Overtown Restaurant. (C)

NATIONAL BANK OF CHESTER COUNTY, WEST CHESTER, PA.

National Bank of Chester County. Bank location is 13 North High Street. The first section was built circa 1789 to 1794. This is another Borough building designed by Thomas Ustick Walter, (1804–1887). The marble mason was Findley Highlands who also was known for his marble work in Founders Hall at Girard College. Unknown publisher but similar to the A. Henry Co. cards, c.1908. (C)

CHAPTER 6

The Inns and Hotels

A few random recent comments and quotations about West Chester's old inns and hotels:

• 1732 Folke Stone: A charming stone manor house, with its open beam ceilings and random width floors was built by Abiah Taylor as a wedding gift for his daughter and son-in-law, Daniel Hoopes

• Faunbrook: 1860s Italian Federal mansion has intricate wrought iron surrounding the wraparound veranda — a great place to sit, looking out over majestic rhododendrons

• Broadlawns: Broadlawns is an 1881 Victorian home touted at the time of its construction as "a grand house and one of the most...beautiful in the borough."

• 1800 Tory Inne: This stone structure, built in 1800, is the former Jesse Reece House and the original General Store and Post Office of Goshenville next to West Chester

• Snug Hollow Farm: Restored 1799 Pennsylvania farm house

• Turk's Head Inn: Since 1769, when the Turk's Head Inn first offered refreshment to weary travelers, West Chester has been a place of hospitality to visitors from around the world

• Crooked Windsor: A charming Victorian bed and breakfast, centrally located in West Chester

The postcards chosen for this chapter reflect the historical look of the town and the key intersections of the borough about one hundred years ago. The town has changed with progress and growth, but some of the old inns and hotels are still quite prominent for all to see and remember the past.

The West Chester Hotel was located at the top of Hannum Ave. at New Street. Jane P. Jeffries opened the hotel in 1828. Jane's husband, John, was one of the proprietors of the Washington Hotel in the center of town. The hotel was torn down to build a municipal parking lot. A scarce Parker and Sons postcard. (D)

The Farmers Hotel was located on the north side of Market St. between New and Darlington Streets. It later became an apartment building and was also torn down to build a parking lot. The Farmers' Hotel is a seldom seen West Chester postcard. (D)

The Eagle Hotel was erected by Jonathan Matlack, c.1803, and was located on the corner of Gay and Walnut Streets. A PMC postcard. (C)

Eagle Hotel in 1909. This Parker and Sons card shows the steam plant of West Chester Electric at the rear of the hotel with its tall smoke smoke stack. The electric plant was located in the 200 block of N. Walnut Street. The hotel was torn down in 1949. (C)

GREEN TREE INN, WEST CHESTER, P.A.   a. H. M.

The Green Tree Inn, built by Isaiah Matlack. It was semi-demolished in 1930. Postcard was used in 1906. The establishment of the courthouse in West Chester led to the erection of several new inns and taverns. Those erected before 1799 include: The Green Tree (1786), The White Hall (1786), The Washington Hotel (1787), and the Black Bear (1789). (C)

Green Tree Inn. Established 1787. West Chester, Pa.

Green Tree Inn, at the corner of Gay and High Streets, with a Moxie sign. A fine Parker and Sons postcard. *Moxie, created in 1876 in Lowell, Massachusetts as a patent medicine by Dr. Augustin Thompson, Moxie was marketed under the product name "Moxie Nerve Food" and was said to cure ailments ranging from softening of the brain to "loss of manhood." In 1884, it was sold in carbonated form and merchandised as an invigorating drink, which claimed to endow the drinker with "spunk." In the early phase of its life as a recreational soft drink, Moxie is said to have been kept handy by bartenders to give to customers who were too drunk to be given any more alcohol.* (C)

GREEN TREE INN, WEST CHESTER, PA. Modern and Up-to-date in all respects   American Plan, $2.00, $2.50 and $3.00 per day.
CHARLES WEINGARTNER, PROP.

Trolley tracks ran right past The Green Tree Inn. Note the Proprietor name and rates on face of Postcard Dist. Co. postcard. (C)

Turk's Head Inn (Established 1768)

West Chester, Pa.

The original name of West Chester was Turk's Head, named after this crossroads tavern of that name. A Parker and Sons postcard. (B)

West Chester was the chosen site for a courthouse and prison to serve a scaled-down Chester County. The Turk's Head Inn was located at High and Market Streets. Phineas Eachus erected the log Turk's Head Tavern on a plot to the south and east of the intersection. The tavern was moved in 1769 by John Hoopes to a brick structure built on a plot south of the original establishment. The location of the new tavern was the northeast corner of present-day High and Market Streets. These were the only improvements up until the American Revolution. But the tavern gave its name to the locality; farmers of the vicinity, when asked where they lived would answer, "Near the Turk's Head Tavern." A. Henry published view. (A)

Turk's Head Inn, West Chester, Pa.

A Fath published card with a nice view of High Street. (C)

A WYCO postcard of the Turk's Head Inn from fairly modern times. (A)

WEST CHESTER,
PA.

MANSION HOUSE,
MARKET AND
CHURCH STS.

The Mansion House
Hotel was built by
William Everhart
in 1831. A Raphael
Tuck & Sons postcard
with notation of Mary
E. Rupert. (C)

The main dining room of
the Mansion House by
Beaux Art publishers. (C)

A colorful artist's
view of the Mansion
House by Miller. (B)

The Tap Room of the Mansion House. A celebrated Beaux Art postcard. (C)

TAP ROOM, MANSION HOUSE HOTEL, WEST CHESTER, PA.

Mansion House, West Chester, Pa.
JOHN R. BOWERS, Proprietor

The Mansion House Hotel was demolished in 1970. Proprietor noted postcard. John R. Bowers in 1913 notation. (C)

The Mansion House breakfast room on this fairly scarce postcard. (C)

Lobby view of the Mansion House. (C)

Merrill postcard with famous "Monkey Cage" in the rear in the Mansion House. (C)

A Goode published view of the lobby. The Mansion House has been a historical land-mark since 1831. (B)

CHAPTER 7

The Courthouse

In 1682 William Penn established Chester County as one of three original counties in the Pennsylvania Colony. Chester County was officially founded in 1683. The first deed was recorded in 1688.

A Court House was constructed in 1724 in Chester near the Delaware River. Population density and migration necessitated moving the facility inland. Between 1784 and 1786 a Court House was built in the village of West Chester on High Street.

In 1846 the Commissioners contracted with Thomas U. Walter to design a structure for the same site. Walter completed his plans for a Greek Revival building and construction began the same year. The brick and stone edifice was opened officially on Washington's birthday, 1848.

Three years later President Millard Fillmore appointed Walter as the Architect of the Capitol, a position that still exists today. Walter designed the Capitol's dome, both the House and Senate wings and other federal buildings.

In 1891 T. Roney Williamson designed the Court House Annex. Built of Indiana limestone, it is an interpretation of the Italian Renaissance style and was erected contiguous to the Greek Revival Court House. The interior was embellished with Italian marble wainscoting; stained art glass; and decorative wood garlands, diamonds, and pilasters.

The Courthouse remains a central focal point in the heart of the lively county seat. The postcards in this section are an endeavor to show the progress of the striking edifice with different observations over moments in time.

Souvenir.
—
West Chester, Pa.,

THE COURT HOUSE.

Chester County Court House. The original court house was built in the village of West Chester on High Street between 1784 and 1786. This is a PMC postcard. (B)

Court House, West Chester, Pa.

Chester County Court House. In 1846 the County Commissioners contracted with Thomas U. Walter to design a structure for the to replace the court house on the same site. Walter completed his plans for a Greek Revival building and construction began the same year. The brick and stone edifice was opened officially on Washington's birthday, 1848. A. Henry postcard. (B)

In 1891 T. Roney Williamson designed the Court House Annex. Built of Indiana limestone, it is an interpretation of the Italian Renaissance style and was erected contiguous to the Greek Revival Court House. The interior was embellished with Italian marble wainscoting; stained art glass; and decorative wood garlands, diamonds, and pilasters. A Raphael Tuck postcard. (B)

WEST CHESTER, PA.
CHESTER COUNTY COURT HOUSE, MARKET AND HIGH STS.

In one block, High Street between Gay and Market Streets, are good specimens of the three great orders of Grecian architecture, designed by Thomas U. Walter, architect of Capitol at Washington: National Bank of Chester County, built, 1836, Doric, white marble; First National Bank, Ionic, white marble; and the Court House, Corinthian, built, 1847 with Pictou stone. An A. Henry postcard. (B)

Chester County Court House, West Chester, Pa.

The crucial event in the evolution of the borough was the 1784 decision to remove the county seat of Chester County from Chester, on the Delaware, to Turk's Head—a more central location for the growing county. West Chester became the county seat in 1788. This is a Fath postcard. (B)

Chester County Court House, West Chester, Pa

West Chester architect T. Roney Williamson manifests the Renaissance Revival in the fine Courthouse Annex of 1893. For imposing effect, the second and third stories are integrated externally and set on the first as a base; a very large cornice crowns the facade with a Chateauesque roof rising above it. Italian workmen dressed the limestone; Italian marble is used within; and the impressive second-floor courtroom is itself Renaissance Revival, with oak paneling and coffered ceiling. A Parker and Sons pre-Old Glory postcard. (B)

CHESTER COUNTY COURT HOUSE, WEST CHESTER, PA.

No doubt it was felt that the dignity of a county seat was compromised by being named for a tavern, and the facts of geography and history dictated the new name. In 1789 "West Chester" was adopted as the name of the new county seat. A Postcard Dist. This postcard is pre "Old Glory". (B)

Soldiers and Sailors Monument Unveiling Day June 11. 1915 West Chester. Pa.

On the Court House lawn is the Soldiers Monument to Civil War patriots, with a bronze figure on a granite base, and erected in 1915. The sculptor was Harry Lewis Raul. Court House postcards are divided by pre-statue/post-statue. Dedication of "Old Glory," a statue of a Civil War soldier holding the American Flag, occurred June 1915. (C)

"OLD GLORY" MONUMENT, CHESTER COUNTY COURT HOUSE, WEST CHESTER, PA.

"Old Glory" shown with two canons that are no longer there on this Postcard Dist. type card. (A)

A Boyer linen type
published postcard
showing "Old Glory,"
c.1913. (A)

W.C.1   Chester County Court House, West Chester, Pa.

8A·H2807

CHESTER COUNTY COURT HOUSE AND SOLDIERS MONUMENT WEST CHESTER, PA

"Old Glory" with cannon view on this fairly uncommon Eagle published card. (C)

CHESTER COUNTY COURT HOUSE, WEST CHESTER, PA.

Today the Court House complex is an assemblage that illustrates Chester County's growth through the decades. The Corinthian columns, designed by Thomas U. Walter, that grace the front entrance have been and will continue to be a distinguishing focal point and symbol of justice far into Chester County's future. The property is listed on the National Register of Historic Places. This is a c.1918 Fath type postcard. (A)

The Chester County Court House on a WYCO-published card in more modern times. (A)

CHAPTER 8
The Hospitals

The Chester County Hospital, established in 1892, is an independent, community-based institution, offering inpatient and outpatient medical/surgical services. Based in West Chester, Pennsylvania, the hospital now has several satellite locations in Exton, Kennett Square and West Chester. At the core of The Health Network of The Chester County Hospital is the century old, 234-bed, not-for-profit hospital. Well known for its comprehensive maternal/child health, oncology, and medical/surgical services, the acute care facility has grown from a small 10-bed dispensary.

The healthcare facilities are depicted on the following postcards, which attempt to reflect the importance of the town's hospitals 100 years ago.

The Homeopathic Hospital, which was also later called the Memorial Hospital, was located in the 300 block of North Walnut Street. The older portion on the right was once the Warrington Mansion. A Fath published card. (Chester County Postcard Album II, Baldwin & Rodebaugh) (B)

The Homeopathic Hospital. Ruben published Photo card in B & W. (C)

Rates are listed on the reverse of this seldom seen postcard of the Marshall Square Sanitarium. As Miss Anna Jarvis, Founder of Mother's Day, grew older and her health declined, her many friends placed her in the Marshall Square Sanitarium in West Chester. It was here that Anna Jarvis died on November 1948 at the age of 84. The West Chester Sanitarium was located in the old Chester County Hospital buildings across from Marshall Square Park. (C)

Parker and Sons postcard view of "The Orchard," Dr. Bayard Kane's 'Sanitariam' postmarked 1910. Dr. Kane's Sanitarium was located on the corner of Old Phoenixville Pike and Fern Hill Road. Dr. Kane was on the staff at Embreeville State Hospital. (D)

Established in 1892, this was Chester County's first hospital. It was situated on the north side of Marshall Street across from Marshall Square Park. (A)

Chester County Hospital, West Chester, Pa.   Henry's Souvenir Card.

61

1912 postmarked view of the growing Chester County Hospital. (B)

The Chester County Hospital has grown from a ten bed dispensary established in 1892 to a provider of a full network of health care services including a 238 bed, not for profit, acute care hospital; home care and many ancillary services. (A)

Construction for the present day hospital began in 1924. Pierre S. DuPont of Wilmington, Delaware, donated almost one million dollars toward the construction of the new hospital. (C)

Chester County Hospital.
This is a Sexichrome card.
(A)

An American Postcard Co. view of Chester County Hospital. In 1900, 9,524 people
lived in West Chester; in 1910, 11,767; and in 1920, 11,717; (A)

A 1909 postmarked view of the hospital, situated on East Marshall Street. (A)

Fath published postcard showing another view of the hospital. (B)

Chester County Hospital. Postcard Distributing Co. card. *Writings were not permitted by law on the address side of any postcard until March 1, 1907. For this reason many postcards up to 1907 have messages across their fronts. Writing on the front of early postcards is not a fault. (B)*

CHESTER COUNTY HOSPITAL, WEST CHESTER, PA.

NEW CHESTER COUNTY HOSPITAL, WEST CHESTER, PA.

Single auto parked in front of the Italian Revival designed Chester County Hospital.
A Fath published card. (B)

Note the new building addition on the right side of the hospital.
This is an E. C. Kropp Co. postcard.
The picture postcard hobby became the greatest collectible hobby that the World has ever known. The official figures from the U.S. Post Office for the fiscal year ending June 30, 1908, cite 677,777,798 postcards mailed. That was at a time when the total population of the U.S. was 88,700,000. (A)

View shows greater expansion of the
Chester County Hospital. (C)

Chester County Hospital.
Merrimack published card
from the 1960s. (B)

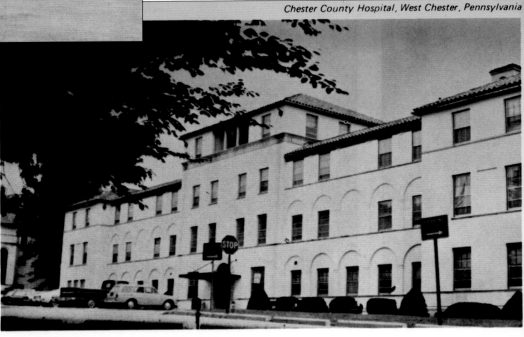

CHAPTER 9
Religious Buildings

It may be a small town but it has "grand classicism." West Chester boasts a wonderful array of religious buildings for worship of classical architecture, designed by such important early Philadelphia architects as William Strickland and Thomas U. Walter.

Today's places of worship include (in random order):

• Baptist Church of West Chester at 221 South High Street
• Emmanuel Baptist Church at 200 South Church Street
• Saint Agnes Church at 233 West Gay Street
• Christian Science Church at 227 North High Street
• Church of God Seventh Day at 234 West Chestnut Street
• Mount Carmel Church of God at 628 East Miner Street
• Holy Trinity Episcopal Church at 212 South High Street
• Calvary Lutheran Church at 730 South New Street
• Bethel AME Church at 334 East Miner Street
• United Methodist Church at 129 South High Street
• Church of the Nazarene at 202 Price Street
• Rock Church of Chester County at 120 East Rosedale Avenue

• First Presbyterian Church at 130 West Miner Street
• Reformed Presbyterian Church at 312 West Union Street
• Beth Chaim Reform Congregation at 123 East Gay Street
• Cornerstone Christian Fellowship at 426 West Gay Street
• Highway Gospel Community Temple at 418 E. Miner Street
• New West Grove Friends Meeting at 217 Sharpless Street
• Rices Temple at 236 East Gay Street
• Second United Presbyterian Church at 114 South Walnut Street
• Seventh Day Adventist Church at 826 South High Street
• St. Luke's UAME Church at 117 South Franklin Street
• Unitarian Fellowship at 501 South High Street
• West Chester Christian Church at 826 South High Street
• West Chester Friends Meeting at 425 North High Street

West Union Street view on a Parker and Sons card. The Church of the Sure Foundation (Reformed Episcopal) was founded in 1884 and was consecrated in 1888. The church portion was torn down before 1960. (C) (*Chester County Postcard Album II*, Baldwin & Rodebaugh)

Church of the Sure Foundation, West Chester, Pa. *Isaiah Chap: 28 verse 16*

Calvary Evangelical Lutheran Church, 750 S. New Street, was formed in 1922 and received its charter in 1924. Services were held at the New Century Club located at High and Lacey Streets from 1925 until 1956. The Church moved to its present location in 1957. A Rochelle published 1958 card of the interior of the Church. (B)

First Baptist Church, West Chester, Pa.

The First Baptist Church located on South High Street is shown without the present day columns on a Parker and Sons postcard. (C)

Market and Darlington Streets location of the Methodist Church was designed by Thomas U. Walter and was built in 1840. The first Methodist Church in West Chester was erected in 1816 and replaced with this more substantial structure. Another Parker and Sons postcard. (C)

The official organization of the First Church of Christ Scientist took place on August 29, 1898, and the first public lecture was given in 1899. The first Church service was held at their lot at 227 North High Street on March 6, 1910. A Parker and Sons card. (B)

Nazarene Tabernacle
Corner Darlington and Dean Sts.
WEST CHESTER, PENNA.
"THE REVIVAL CHURCH"
[SEE OTHER SIDE]

The First Church of the Nazarene, Price and Darlington Sts., was organized June 6, 1928 with 28 charter members including a Darlington and a Dean. The spiritual vision of early Nazarenes was derived from the doctrinal core of John Wesley's preaching and the holiness movement. The Church of the Nazarene was founded in 1895 in Los Angeles, California by Phineas Bresee. Bresee, was a former Methodist minister. (C)

The Second Presbyterian Church, 114 S. Walnut Street, started as a mission Sunday school at the First Presbyterian Church in October 1880. A rarely seen Craven published postcard. (D)

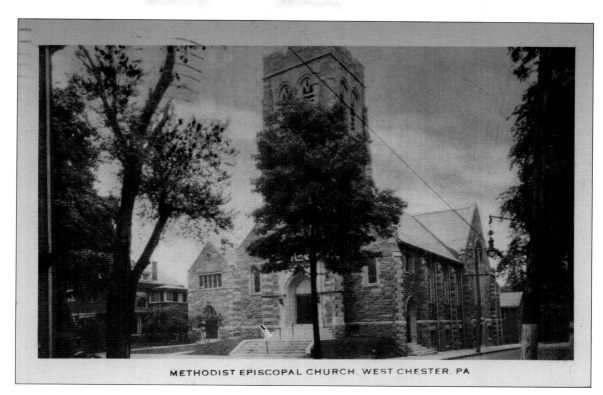

METHODIST EPISCOPAL CHURCH, WEST CHESTER, PA

The Methodist Episcopal Church, now the United Methodist Church of West Chester built this Gothic style edifice at
129 South High St. in 1919. 1926 postmarked view on an
Eagle published card. (C)

A Fath card showing the Methodist Episcopal Church. (A)

St. Agnes Catholic Church, West Chester, Pa.

Christ's Church, at 223 West Gay Street, was founded about 1793. The building, which later became St. Agnes Church, stood on a grassy knoll on West Gay Street. The Church dedicated to St. Agnes the virgin and martyr was built in 1852. Oval postcard by Parker and Sons. (D)

The first services at Holy Trinity were held on January 23, 1870. The parish building was consecrated on December 6, 1882 and the tower, bells and memorial windows were added in 1888. (A)

Built in 1857 with the tower dating from 1890, serpentine quarry stone was used in the construction of this stately Holy Trinity church located at 210 S. High Street. (corner of High and Union Streets). Two serpentine stone quarries operated in the southwestern corner of Westtown near West Chester. These quarries provided most of the stone for early buildings in the area. In the 1880s, up to 40 people were employed at "Brinton's Quarry." Much of the stone was hauled to the railroad station. The stone was used in churches throughout the northeastern United States. In 1888, a fire destroyed the buildings and water pumps of the quarry, and the quarrying was discontinued. This is a Raphael Tuck produced postcard. (B)

WEST CHESTER, PA. CHURCH OF THE HOLY TRINITY, SO. HIGH ST.

Printed in Germany

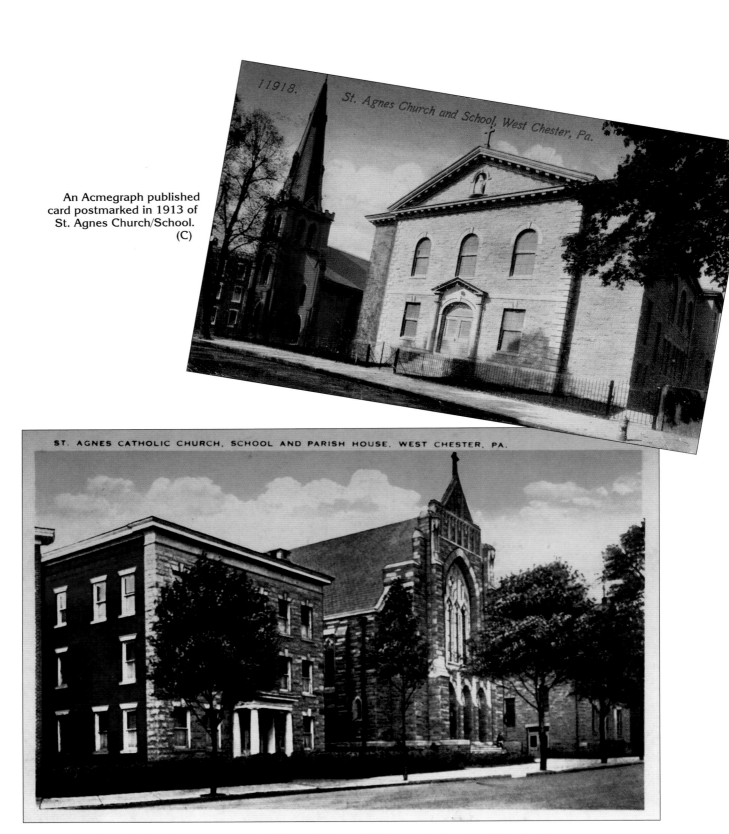

An Acmegraph published card postmarked in 1913 of St. Agnes Church/School. (C)

The new Gothic style church was erected in 1925-26. Prior to 1812 the only church building for Roman Catholics in West Chester was a miniature one, erected in 1793 where now stands the present edifice. The first church was a one-story brick structure containing three windows on each side with a front door facing west. It accommodated 150 people. This is a Fath postcard. (C)

First Presbyterian Church and Chapel, West Chester, Pa.

Abbie M. Atkins. May 28. 1909

Thomas U. Walterdesigned this First Presbyterian Church situated at Miner and Darlington Streets at a young age. The First Presbyterian Church of West Chester was founded in 1834. A. Henry postcard. (A)

The First Presbyterian Church, West Chester, Pennsylvania

An interior view of First Presbyterian Church on a Graycraft card. (B)

First Presbyterian Church, West Chester, Pa.

Construction of this First Presbyterian Church, 130 W. Miner Street, began July 3, 1832, but was not completed until January 1834. The Church was designed by Thomas U. Walter, who also designed the dome of the Capitol building in Washington D.C. This is a card published by Diamond "W". (A)

Catholic Convent and Chapel, West Chester, Pa.

The foundation of Villa Maria dates back to July 1872 when the Sisters of the Immaculate Heart of Mary were transferred from Reading, Pennsylvania to West Chester. The property between N. Penn St and Marshall Streets was formerly owned by the Pennsylvania Military Academy. It flourished in West Chester until 1914. This is an American News Co. postcard. (A)

VILLA MARIA, WEST CHESTER, PA.—INTERIOR OF CHAPEL.

Interior view of the chapel at Villa Maria in 1909. It was located at 700 West Marshall Street. (C)

VILLA MARIA CONVENT, WEST CHESTER, PA.

Villa Maria Convent on a Rotograph postcard.
A popular publisher the Rotograph Postcard Co. waw located in New York City and Chicago. This company published as many as 60,000 different postcards dealing with a variety of subjects ranging from scenic views of towns and cities to real photos. (A)

St. Anthony's Grotto, Villa Maria, West Chester, Pa.

St. Aanthony's grotto was located on the Marshall Street side of the convent. St. Anthony is the patron saint of lost items, the poor and travelers. (Courtesy of Donna Naylor-White). (D)

Westminster Presbyterian Church
West Chester, Pa.
Rev. C. R. Williamson, Ph.D., Pastor

Westminster Presbyterian Church was founded in 1892 and for over 100 years the church was in downtown West Chester at Church and Barnard Streets. Card lists the pastor. (C)

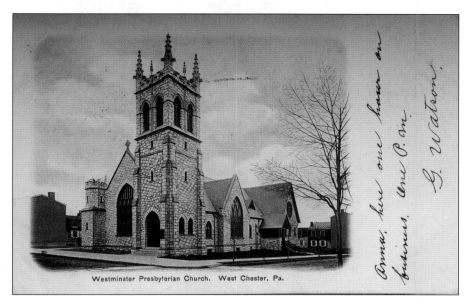

Westminster Presbyterian Church. 1907 postmarked card
published by the American News Co. (B)

Olivet Baptist Church; 1897-1919. The
Olivet Baptist Church was organized in
1897. The First Baptist Church and the
Olivet Baptist Church merged in 1929.
The building is now home to the Re-
formed Presbyterian Church. (C)

A Henry published card
with vintage auto in front
of the Olivet Baptist
Church located at 312
West Union Street. (A)

Olivet Baptist Church. Rotograph Co. postcard. (A)

THE BAPTIST CHURCH OF WEST CHESTER, PA.

The Baptist Church of West Chester, located at 221 South High Street. The First Baptist Church of West Chester was formed on December 23, 1833, and the Church was built in 1836. The First Baptist Church and the Olivet Baptist Church merged in 1929. The church became The Baptist Church of West Chester. (B)

Right:
The First Baptist Church was established in 1833 in West Chester. This is a Goode card. (A)

THE BAPTIST CHURCH OF WEST CHESTER, P.A.

The Baptist Church is located a half-mile north of West Chester University
and a quarter-mile south from the center of the Borough. (B)

CHAPTER 10
Quaker Buildings

West Chester was settled in the early 18th century, principally by members of the Society of Friends.

King Charles II owed William Penn £16,000, money which Admiral Penn had lent him. Seeking a haven in the New World for persecuted Friends, Penn asked the King to grant him land in the territory between Lord Baltimore's province of Maryland and the Duke of York's province of New York. With the Duke's support, Penn's petition was granted. The King signed the Charter of Pennsylvania on March 4, 1681, and it was officially proclaimed on April 2. The King named the new colony in honor of William Penn's father. It was to include the land between the 39th and 42nd degrees of north latitude and from the Delaware River westward for five degrees of longitude. Other provisions assured its people the protection of English laws and, to a certain degree, kept it subject to the government in England. Provincial laws could be annulled by the King. In 1682 the Duke of York deeded to Penn his claim to the three lower counties on the Delaware, which are now the state of Delaware.

The respected Society of Friends has been uniquely identified with the state of Pennsylvania since the days of its founder, William Penn. The first settlement of the Society of Friends in the state appears to have been at Uniontown in about 1769.

West Chester Friends School is a Quaker day school serving the needs of 135 students from Early Start (age 4) through Grade 5. Established in 1836 under the care of West Chester Monthly Meeting of the Religious Society of Friends, the school is located in the borough of West Chester.

Friends Meeting House, 50 West Chestnut Street. William Penn's colony chartered in 1681 by King Charles II to Penn, a Quaker, Pennsylvania received her new governor aboard the Welcome the following year. The new immigrants were primarily English Quakers, although some were of Welsh, Scottish, and Irish ancestry. An American Postcard Co. card view. (C)

WEST CHESTER, PA. FRIENDS MEETING HOUSE, W. CHESTNUT ST.

Mary E. Rupert, West Chester, Pa.

Printed in Germany.

Friends Meeting House, A Raphael Tuck published postcard with the Rupert notation. (B)

Friends Meeting House,
Built 1810, West Chester, Pa.

The Chester Meeting, founded in 1681, was descended from the Burlington (NJ) Meeting (founded 1678), and during 1810, the West Chester meeting was founded from its descendants. Rotograph Co. postcard. (A)

Many Quakers were Irish and Welsh, and they settled in the area immediately outside of Philadelphia (Chester County). Parker and Sons postcard postmarked in 1907. (C)

FRIENDS' MEETING-HOUSE, HIGH STREET, WEST CHESTER, PA.
Earliest house 1813. Extensive alterations 1867-8.

One of the best-known 20th century African American Quakers was Bayard Rustin, who was one of the most important leaders of the American civil rights movement from the advent of its modern period, in the 1950s, until well into the 1980s. Bayard was born in West Chester in 1912. His maternal grandparents were Friends and Quakerism became his faith. A view of 400 North High Street. (C)

HIGH STREET FRIENDS' MEETING HOUSE, WEST CHESTER, PA.

The Friends School of West Chester was founded in 1800. Established in 1836 under the care of West Chester Monthly Meeting of the Religious Society of Friends, the school is located in historic West Chester. A Tichnor Bros., Inc. published card postmarked in 1924. (A)

FRIENDS' MEETING HOUSE, West Chester, Pa.

The Friends School of West Chester. William Penn was born in London on October 24, 1644, the son of Admiral Sir William Penn. Despite high social position and an excellent education, he shocked his upper-class associates by his conversion to the beliefs of the Society of Friends, or Quakers, then a persecuted sect. Parker and Sons view with a 1911 postmark. (B)

Friends Meeting House. Dock split frame type postcard showing interior and exterior views. (C)

High Street Friends Meeting House.
West Chester, Pa.

11916.

Josiah Hoopes' church, the West Chester Meeting, founded in 1810, was descended from the Birmingham Meeting (founded 1694), which was in turn descended from the Concord Mmeeting (1684), the Chester Meeting (1681) and the Burlington (NJ) Meeting (1678). An Acmegraph card with a 1913 postmark. (B)

West Chester Friends School is a Quaker day school situated at 400 North High Street, serving the needs of 135+ students from Early Start (age 4) through Grade 5. Established in 1836 under the care of West Chester Monthly Meeting of the Religious Society of Friends. This postcard was published by American News.Co. (A)

Friends School and Meetinghouse, West Chester, Pa.

Friends Meeting House (built 1864), West Chester, Pa.

The first Friend's Meeting was established in West Chester in 1810. They met in a private home, but began to build a regular meetinghouse on North High Street in 1812 and used it for the first time in 1813. It was enlarged in 1868. Parker and Sons view. (C)

Hicksite Friends Meeting House, West Chester, Pa.

The Hicksite division affected West Chester as well, and the Orthodox Friends separated from the original meeting in 1830. They built their own meetinghouse at the corner of Church and Chestnut Streets. In 1844, they built a stone meetinghouse on the northeast corner of that intersection. This is a Henry-published card. (C)

CHAPTER 11
Monuments *and* Parks

West Chester has three major parks Everhart Park, Hoopes Park, and Marshall Square Park, and eight (8) smaller neighborhood parks. These parks are dispersed throughout the Borough. They offer a variety of prospects for active and passive recreation, and help to enhance the quality of life in the immediate neighborhoods.

Marshall Square Park was modeled after Washington Square Park in Philadelphia. Botanizing was a favorite avocation of West Chester's professional men, some of who attained international recognition. Dr. William Darlington, Joshua Hoopes, and David Townsend were such botanizers, and they succeeded in having this square developed as a small arboretum. In 1878 it became a public park, based on a plan by Joshua Hoopes, a nurseryman.

Although most of its large and exotic trees are gone, a few remain, and it is of value to walk through the park to find them. The southwest corner originally held a basin for West Chester's water supply; now it features the Soldiers' Monument honoring the 97th Regiment of the Civil War.

Its founders named the square after the 18th century botanist Humphry Marshall. Marshall was born in 1722 and never went to school after the age of twelve; yet (appropriately for a cousin of William Bartram, America's most celebrated explorer/botanist) he published in 1785 *Arbustum Americanum, the American Grove.*

New Century Fountain, Stolen from West Chester, Pa.

The New Century Fountain cast in 1898 by a local sculptress, Martha G. Cornwell, is a stolen object of art. An Eric C. Wilson card. (B)

New Century Fountain, N. High St., West Chester. Pa.   Henry's Souvenir Card.

The fountain was stolen during a snowstorm in the late 1950s. The 1.8-square-mile borough is home to 11 parks. A Henry published card. (A)

Everhart Fountain, W. Market St., West Chester, Pa.   Henry's Souvenir Card.

[[[The image is of the Everhart fountain on market street. What is the connection to the park, other than the name???]]] **One of Borough's most beautiful parks is Everhart Park, located on the west side of town south of Miner Street between Brandywine Street and Bradford Avenue. Everhart Grove became West Chester's second public park in November 1905.** (A)

Marshall Square. Parker and Sons card postmarked in 1910. (B)

A Henry published card
showing the park and
fountain named after
the famous botanist Mr.
Humphrey Marshall.
(B)

1A971

Nice view of Marshall Square on this Boyer card. (B)

MARSHALL SQUARE, WEST CHESTER, PA.

Postmarked 1927 card showing another view of the monument on the Square. A Fath published card. (A)

Everhart Park, West Chester, Pa.

Everhart Park. William Everhart (1785-1868) was born in Pennsylvania. He was the father of James Bowen Everhart, U.S. Representative from Pennsylvania's 6th District, 1853-55, and died in 1868. William's interment is in Oakland Cemetery near the borough of West Chester. A Parker and Sons card postally utilized in 1907. (B)

Everhart Park, West Chester, Pa

Parker and Sons postcard showing shed at Everhart Park. Everhart's accomplishments deserve more attention. He built more than one hundred buildings in West Chester including its most fashionable hotel, a very successful dry goods store, and its first permanent farmers market. He also laid out Market Street, as well as four residential streets named after his friends Isaac Wayne, General Barnard, Charles Miner, and Dr. William Darlington. (B)

Council resolved to "tender Dr. Isaiah F. Everhart, our most sincere thanks for his most magnanimous gift of all that portion of ground known as Everhart's Grove and adjoining property as set forth in the deed, to the Borough of West Chester, Pa. Said property to be used as a public park. By this magnificent gift will be perpetuated the honored name of Everharts who resided in this Borough and whose efforts were instrumental in building a foundation for our Borough that will be a lasting tribute. The donor of this generous gift will ever be honored and revered by the citizens of our Borough, and to him are the residents of West Chester duly thankful." (B)

General View in Park showing Summer House, West Chester, Pa.

PERGOLA, EBERHARDT PARK, WEST CHESTER, PA.

A large heavily treed park in the western section of the Borough, Everhart Park is used for concerts and other outdoor activities and events. (A)

3 EBERHART GROVE PARK, WEST CHESTER, PA

This is a misidentified Everhart Park postcard. The park is located between Miner and Union Streets and by Bradford Avenue and Brandywine Street. A lovely park still used by the residents of West Chester. (B)

FOUNTAIN, EBERHARDT PARK, WEST CHESTER, PA.

Everhart Park view, though the name is misspelled. C. T. Photochrome Co. card. (B)

Monument to the 97th R. V.
West Chester, Pa.

Spot Where Lafayette Was Wounded, Brandywine Battlefield
Near Westchester, Pa.

Tribute to Lafayette, Revolutionary War hero. (A)

Memorial to the 97th PA Volunteers. Authority from the Secretary of War to recruit a regiment for three years came in 1861 Enrolling was immediately commenced and in two months time its ranks were full. Companies D and I were principally from Delaware County, and the remaining companies were principally from Chester County. The companies rendezvoused and Camp Wayne, near the borough of West Chester and were organized under the following field officers: Henry R. Guss, Colonel; Augustus P. Duer, Lieutenant Colonel; Galusha Pennypacker, Major. Clothing, arms and equipment were furnished from the arsenal in Philadelphia. This is a Kirby postcard. (B)

Rural scene that is almost a Wyeth-like view is situated in the northeast section of West Chester. (A)

West Chester Community Center. Artvue Post Card Co. postcard, of 225 Fifth Ave. New York, N.Y. *The Golden Age of Postcards was from 1898 to 1918.* (C)

CHAPTER 12
Schools

The provision of education in early America for the poor was a favorite Quaker philanthropy. As one historian has pointed out, "the poor, both Quaker and non-Quaker, were allowed to attend without paying fees."

In the countryside around Philadelphia, including West Chester, German immigrants and Quakers maintained many of their own schools. By 1776, at least sixteen schools were being operated by the Mennonites in Eastern Pennsylvania.

Historical facts about West Chester's schools:

• The Friends School of West Chester was founded in 1800.

• Joshua Hoopes opened the "Downingtown Boarding School For Boys" in 1817, moved it to West Chester in 1834, and closed it in 1862.

• The plans to build the West Chester Railroad led to the construction of Price's Boarding School for young ladies in 1830. By 1857, it was flourishing under Ms. Evans.

• In 1871 The Sisters of the Immaculate Heart of Mary founded the Villa Maria

• In 1914, the Villa Maria Academy moved from West Chester to its present location at Immaculata and was chartered by the state of Pennsylvania in 1921.

• The Darlington Seminary opened in 1901.

Darlington Seminary, West Chester, Pa.

The Darlington Seminary was located just west of the Borough line on W. Miner. (*Images of America, West Chester*, Martha Carson-Gentry and Paul Rodebaugh 1997) The Darlington Seminary (nonsectarian; for girls), founded in 1851 by Smedley Darlington (1827-1899), who was the principal of the school from 1851 to 1861 and was a representative in Congress in 1887-1891. This is a Parker and Sons card postmarked in 1912. (C)

The Darlington Seminary operated in West Chester under Superintendent Frank B. Bye, from 1901 until at least 1926. A stereo view, bi-fold postcard by Kirby. (C)

The Darlington Seminary was called Ercildoun Seminary when it began in 1851. It was originally a boy's school. but it soon changed to an all-girls school. Postmarked Sexichrome card dated 1924. (B)

In the summer of 1877, after the school was destroyed by a tornado that struck its original site, Richard Darlington moved the Ercildoun Seminary to a location just outside of West Chester and renamed it the Darlington Seminary. A Henry-published card. (B)

"The Darlington," residence of the Byes. A Hedgley postcard, postmarked 1906. (B)

West Chester High School, 50 W. Biddle St., graduated its first class in 1866 and occupied this building from 1863 until 1906. The school was torn down and some of its bricks were used for the new High School located at the corner of Biddle and Church Streets. This is a PMC card dated 1905. (C)

The West Chester High School at Church and Biddle Sts. was built in 1906 and was destroyed by fire in December, 1947. This is a fine Henry postcard. (B)

High School,
West Chester, Pa.

The original High School can be seen to the left. Another historical view by Kirby.
West Chester earned the reputation of the "Athens of Pennsylvania" during the first half of the nineteenth century because of her educational institutions, her Greek Revival architecture, and her many learned societies. The first of many private schools to be established here was the West Chester Academy, founded in 1813. Among the other early private schools were Price's Boarding School for Girls (1830), Almira Lincoln Phelps Young Ladies Seminary (1837), and Bolmar's Academy (1840). (A)

Right:
The Gay Street School (later Fugett School) was built in 1894 for $25,000. It had seven teachers and a principal. It was renovated in 1910 and rebuilt in 1956. A Henry Co. postcard. (*Images of America, West Chester,* Martha Carson-Gentry and Paul Rodebaugh - 1997) (B)

The Gay St. Public School, 400 E. Gay Street, was built in 1895 from the design by Arthur Willauer. The school was built primarily for African-American Students. The school was destroyed by fire in 1908, and a new school was built; it was integrated in 1957. The building became the Borough Hall in the 1990s and has since been razed and is now a parking area for the new Municipal Building. Parker and Sons card postmarked 1909. (*Images of America, West Chester,* Martha Carson-Gentry and Paul Rodebaugh - 1997) (C)

HIGH STREET PUBLIC SCHOOL,

A 3753 Li▮▮▮▮▮▮▮▮▮▮▮▮▮▮▮▮ West Chester, Pa.

This postcard is an error card from the Rotograph Company. It was originally printed as "Library, State Normal School." When the mistake was realized, a 'blackout' stamp was used to correct it to read High Street Public School. (C)

The High Street School, 400 S. High Street, was built in 1889 from a design by T. Roney Williamson. This building was torn down in 1978 and is now a Burger King. A Henry-published card. (B)

St. Agnes Church and School, 200 W. Gay St. The original Church was erected in 1853 and was replaced by the current Church building in 1926. A Roman Catholic congregation was first established in West Chester in 1793. A Sexichrome card. (C)

St. Agnes Parochial School was erected in 1910, at 211 West Gay Street. This is a Photochrome postcard. (C)

The Villa Maria Academy, 700 N. Penn St., stood on property formerly owned by the Pennsylvania Military Academy. Seven Oaks Apartments now stands on the property. The foundation of the academy dates to July 1872. At that time, the Sisters, Servants of the Immaculate Heart of Mary transferred their motherhouse, novitiate, and boarding school from Reading to West Chester. The school flourished in West Chester until 1914, when Villa Maria moved to Immaculata. Having a blend of educational excellence and Christian values, begun more than 130 years ago in West Chester, the school flourishes today at the present site in Malvern. An American Postcard Co view. (A)

In 1914, the Villa Maria Academy moved from West Chester to its present location at Immaculata, Pennsylvania and was chartered by the state of Pennsylvania in 1921. This is a W. A. Pierce card postally marked 1917.
In December 1861, Philadelphia businessman John P. Charlton copyrighted the design of a private postal card, with a border round the card and lines on one side for the address and the stamp. He went into business with the local printer, Hyman L Lipman and the card carried the message "Lipman's Postal Card, patent applied for." However (and perhaps not surprisingly) no patent appears to have been granted. The rarity of such cards suggests the idea was not commercially successful. (C)

CHAPTER 13
Normal School

West Chester University traces its ancestry back to September 28, 1811. Under the leadership of Dr. William Darlington, a group of men met in the Chester County Court House to establish an educational institution. On March 27, 1812, a charter of five articles drawn by Dr. Darlington resulted in the incorporation of the West Chester Academy.

A public meeting was held on August 3, 1869 at the Court House for anyone interested in establishing a normal school in West Chester to provide teachers for Chester, Delaware, Montgomery, and Bucks counties.

In 1913 West Chester became the first of the normal schools to be owned by the Commonwealth.

West Chester Normal School became West Chester State Teachers College in 1927, when it offered a four-year program for liberal arts.

The postcards depicting the Normal School are numerous and the following postcards are a selection highlighting the school from an historical viewpoint.

West Chester Academy opened in 1813. Mr. William F. Wyers became the principal on March 11, 1854. After the Civil War, the Academy folded into the West Chester Normal School, the fore-runner of West Chester University. A rarely seen Digby postcard showing the Purple and Gold colors of the school. The purple and gold school colors were officially adopted on May 25, 1892.
(C)

West
Chester State
Normal School

WEST CHESTER, PA.   STATE NORMAL SCHOOL.

"Old Main." The corner stone for this building was laid on September 14, 1870. The structure was de-signed to be built with Briton's Quarry Serpentine stone. Serpentine or "green Stone" is a metamorphic crystalline rock found principally in Chester county and northern Maryland. Old Main was demolished in 1971. The university has never been larger than at present, but its growth occurred in very distinct stages. The first major expansion took place before World War One during the tenure of Principal George M. Philips (1881-1920). A PMC card. (C)

Right:
Philips Memorial Hall is the symbolic front door to West Chester University. Designed by Price and Walton in 1925, it houses the university's main auditorium, a rare book library, lecture halls, meeting rooms, and the president's office. It is located on the corner of High St. and College Ave. Named after George M. Philips, who was the Principal from 1881-1920. An Eagle published card. (C)

Posting area history

Two local men share
their love of postcards
and West Chester in
recently published book

By JUSTIN McANENY
Staff Writer

I f a picture is worth a thousand
words, then "West Chester History, A Review in Early Postcards," doesn't cost enough. Like
all towns across the country, West
Chester progressed through the
ages. Changes were made that
aren't always known: hotels torn
down, statues erected, roads
paved, a trolley connected West
Chester to Philadelphia. It wasn't
always like it is today.

William Schultz and Robert
Sheller created the book on West
Chester for younger generations
who might not be familiar with the
borough's history, to capture a
glimpse of time that some might remember and also share their love
of postcards.

The book is a collection of 275
postcards that were created in the
early part of the 20th century,
"From about 1902 to 1920,"
Schultz said. Sheller added that

Three commercial truck drivers put on the brakes to help police stop a man who led authorities on a high-speed chase for more than 30 miles in Biggs Ore.

The truckers pulled alongside each other and slowed to about 5 mph, forming a rolling road block. The fleeing driver stopped and ran away but was quickly captured, authorities said.

Trucker Edwin Beach said he had heard police radio traffic and said, "OK, where's the high-speed chase at?" He coordinated with two other drivers over CB and placed his truck in the middle on Interstate 84.

"We were all kind of laughing because he was running down the freeway," said Beach, of Kelso, Wash. Identities of the other two truckers were not immediately available.

The chase began Saturday near Boardman and ended near the John Day Dam on the Columbia River about 100 miles east of Portland, police said. Speeds during the chase exceeded 100 mph.

The fleeing car had been reported to have been involved in a hit-and-run.

The man who currently holds the world's record for the tallest sand castle is pouring cold sea water on Myrtle Beach, S.C.'s, attempt to dethrone him.

Ed Jarrett, from Casco, Maine, said the 43-foot castle built in June in Myrtle Beach failed to follow Guinness World Records guidelines that ban using machinery and require the structure to be taller than it is wide.

"Myrtle Beach doesn't meet the criteria," Jarrett said. "You can't just pile up a bunch of sand, build a small castle on top of that pile, and call it a record."

He said his nearly 32-foot-tall castle, completed last weekend in Maine, should be the new record holder.

Myrtle Beach officials had permission from Guinness to stray from the guidelines, said Holly McMillan, a spokeswoman for the Myrtle Beach Area Chamber of Commerce.

"It's unsafe to have a structure that tall without a base to support it, and Guinness recognized that," McMillan said. "We also told Guinness that the city would not allow us to hand deliver the sand, and they said it would be OK to use machinery to bring the sand castle in."

The Guinness organization hasn't yet decided whether the Myrtle Beach castle should be considered an official record.

Police horses may be allowed freedom

The Madison, Wis., city pooper-scooper law annul...

Associated Press

Winter, a tailless dolphin, rests on her mat at the Clearwater Marine Aquarium in Clearwater, Fla.

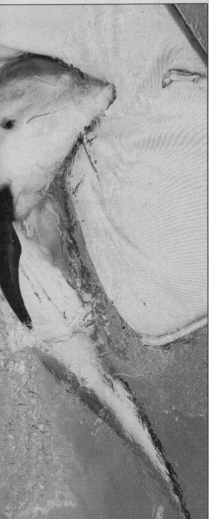

Dolphin receives prosthetic tail

By PHIL DAVIS
Associated Press Writer

Prosthetic specialist Kevin Carroll travels the country tackling the toughest human amputation cases, so it was only natural that he was also drawn to Winter — the only known dolphin to survive the loss of her powerful tail flukes.

"My heart went out to her, and I was thinking I could probably put a tail on her," said Carroll, vice president of prosthetics at Hanger Orthopedic Group, Inc of Clearwater, Fla.

Recreating one of the most powerful swimming mechanisms in nature turned out to be a lot tougher than expected. But after months of experimenting, Carroll and a unique team of experts are well on their way to, as one of them puts it, "MacGyvering" a tail for Winter.

Unlike the 1980s cult TV hero "MacGyver," who worked his way out of tight spots with

Lessons can also be learned that will help human amputees. Carroll, for example, found the gel sleeve he developed to cling to 18-month-old Winter's tail without irritating her sensitive skin also soothed a painful prothesis for Air Force Senior Airman Brian Kolfage, who lost both legs and his right hand in a 2004 mortar attack in Iraq. The sleeve sticks to Winter's tail with suction the same way a rubber surgical glove grips a human hand.

"When he tried to walk with prosthetics, you had these dagger-like boney growths sticking into the socket. It was very painful," Carroll said. "Brian's situation was similar to Winter's. Winter helped him and hopefully she'll help a lot of others as well."

Carroll, an Orlando resident whose company is based in Bethesda, Md., said he is already thinking of new materials to make human prosthetics tougher in saltwater. And Walsh said the research on Winter is invaluable for understanding dolphin physiology and the treatment of back injuries, which can occur

"We put together a team who doesn't know what 'no' means," said Mike Walsh, Winter's lead veterinarian and a program manager at the University of Florida's aquatic animal health program. "As long as you're willing to try, you can make a big difference."

Aquarium, a nonprofit marine animal rescue center and popular local attraction located in the Gulf Coast city's former water treatment plant.

◆ See TAIL, Page C3

cers on mounted patrol a... K-9 unit duty – but a ne... statute may allow them t... start leaving the evidence b... hind.

An ordinance amendmen... to be taken up Tuesday ... aimed at making it easier fo... the city to increase its use o... mounted police patrols.

Alderwomen Judy Comp... ton and Lauren Cnare, co...

His 29-foot castle is the current record holder and he spent about two months building the 32-foot-tall castle with the help of 1,500 volunteers to raise money for a retreat for children with life-threatening illnesses.

"I spent four years engineering this castle, and these volunteers worked their butts off to get the record,"

History

(From Page C1)

more collectors and are hoping that people will come forward with post cards they haven't seen before.

"I think the baby boomers have found post-cards," Schultz said.

– To find out more information on "West

Chester His... cards," visit... – On Satu... and 2 p.m. by Robert... Chadds Fo... Ford. – To conta... send an e-m... or visit his philly.com/b... blog.html.

Ladies
Back to School

Learn the ABC's of

Thursday, September 20 6-9 p.m.

Introducing Citadel's
New Checking Accounts!

Citadel

★ Citadel FREE Checking
★ Citadel STAR Checking(SM)
★ Citadel STAR Premiere Checking(SM)

And the winner is...
You!

Featuring:
• Higher Interest Rates
• ID Theft Protection

Sheller's home in West Goshen. Below are some of the pages in the book depicting advertising cards for Sharples Separators.

color to the book.

Schultz and Sheller agree that there are probably more than 1,000 different postcards of West Chester that were created in the early part of the previous century. And between the two men, they probably have most of them — or at least all the ones they know about.

"They were used like e-mail," Schultz said. "Postcards were the earliest form of e-mail."

Schultz explained that postcards were often sent between family members as quick greetings and as a way to let each other know that if you were on a trip, or in school, that everything was OK. He added that they could be brief, with just one word like "hello," and they were "almost always relative to relative."

But before there was the book, there was the friendship.

Schultz and Sheller met "four or five years ago." They used to bid on postcards against each other on eBay or at auctions. And in passing had mentioned to each other that it would be interesting to write a book on postcards. But it never happened.

"Schiffer (Publishing, based in Atglen) called us," Sheller said. Well, they called Schultz — who, after he was convinced it wasn't a hoax — thought of Sheller. "I knew," said Schultz, "working together ... we would put out a better product."

"I wondered, 'Where's the gimmick?'" Sheller said.

But it wasn't.

According to Schultz, collecting postcards is the fastest-growing hobby in the United States. And West Chester is full of history. Sheller, a retired West Chester Police officer who has lived in and around the borough his entire life, and Schultz, who moved to the West Chester area in 1974 — both being avid collectors for most of their lives — were the ones to write the book.

The next steps were for Sheller and Schultz to figure out the direction of the book and even harder — which postcards would make it into the book.

The book has 14 chapters, with each one focusing on a specific theme or place in West Chester: main streets, architecture, the courthouse, "The Normal School" (which is now known as West Chester University).

One of Sheller's favorite chapters is the one on architecture. "I love the views," he said. Sheller, who loves the front of the postcards is complimented by Schultz.

Schultz is a "well known postal historian and nationally accredited philatelic judge. Sheller said, "Bill knows the who, what and where the card went ... the back of the cards."

Sheller also likes that if you look at the cards closely, you can try to figure out what the differences between then and now are. Like, there is a postcard in the book with a picture of the West Chester Courthouse. When the picture was taken, the statue "Old Glory" that is in front of the courthouse wasn't there when the picture was taken.

"There are cards that are almost 100 years old in the book. ... We captured the history of West Chester 100 years ago," Schultz said.

And what separates their book from others is that there is a price index so that you can see how much each card is worth.

Now that the book is out, Sheller and Schultz are hoping to find

◆ See HISTORY, Page C2

A classic pose on this advertising postcard published by Sharples. (C)

In 1988, Sharples and Alfa Laval once again joined forces to form the largest and most advanced separation company in the world. Today, the Alfa Laval separators are a significant part of Alfa Laval's agricultural dairy ... (A)

ENTRANCE PHILIP'S MEMORIAL CHAPEL
STATE TEACHERS COLLEGE WEST CHESTER, PA

A 3749 Cottage, State Normal School, West Chester, Pa.

Dr. Philips's resdence. During the period prior to World War One, the Normal School acquired thirty-six additional acres, and constructed an addition to Old Main (1889), a gymnasium (1890), the principal's house ("Green Gables," finished in 1891), Recitation Hall (1892) and the "Sanitarium" (1892), the "Model School" (Ruby Jones Hall, in 1899), and the Old Library (1902). Located on the northwest corner of High Street. and College Avenue (once called Normal Ave.), it was Dr. Philips residence and later used as the college president's home. A Rotograph Co. card. (B)

The Model School (later the "Demonstration School") opened on the West Chester Normal School campus in 1898. Its building, later named Ruby Jones Hall, is located in the 50 block of College Avenue. It officially opened on December 4, 1899. The seniors used it as a place where they could practice to teach. Enrollment grew during the early part of the century, and in 1901 the Normal School graduated 166 students, up from ten in 1874. In order to house everyone, the school opened Wayne Hall, an all-male dormitory, built on Wayne Field near Church Street and West Rosedale Avenue in 1911. American News Co. postcard. (B)

Model Building, State Normal School. West Chester, Pa.

A full view of the school This birds eye view shows the Model School building, Gymnasium, Recitation Hall, Old Main, the Library, Wayne Hall, and the baseball field. (B)

Classic view of Old Main, designed by Addison Hutton, on the campus. Although its founding year is 1871, the University in fact has deeper roots going back to the West Chester Academy, a private, state-aided school that existed from 1812 to 1869. The academy enjoyed strong support from the highly intellectual Chester County Cabinet of the Natural Sciences of the pre-Civil War decades. It was recognized as one of Pennsylvania's leading preparatory schools, and its experience in teacher training laid the groundwork for the normal school years. A WYCO postcard. (A)

The Boys Dormitory was also called Wayne Hall. It was built in 1911 with serpentine stone. The building was demolished around 1969. The normal school admitted its first class, consisting of 160 students, on September 25, 1871. A Sexichrome postcard. (B)

VIEW FROM TENNIS COURTS

This is a card published by Horace F. Temple who was a local West Chester printer. (A)

Looking south on campus. This view was taken before Anderson Hall was built on the site. A Photostint card. (B)

Recitation Hall, State Normal School, West Chester, Pa.

Recitation Hall was also built with serpentine stone. This postcard has a 1912 postmark. (A)

Students mugging for the camera behind Recitation Hall on campus. In recognition of the historic merit of the campus, in 1981 the West Chester State College Quadrangle Historic District was placed on the National Register of Historic Places. The buildings included in this historic district are Philips Memorial Building, Ruby Jones Hall, Recitation Hall, and the Old Library. Except for Philips, these buildings are all constructed of native Chester County serpentine stone. A photo type card. (D)

Library Building of State Normal School, West Chester, Pa.

The Old Library. West Chester became West Chester State Teachers College in 1927 when Pennsylvania initiated a four-year program of teacher education. An American News postcard. (B)

INTERIOR OF THE LIBRARY—STATE NORMAL SCHOOL

Old Library (constructed in 1902) interior view. The original library was in "Old Main." Postmarked 1910 (C)

In front of the library in 1910. Rare, light green natural bedrock, serpentine is believed to have been thrust up from the earth's core during plate shifting activity some 450 million years ago. Found only in a few places around the globe including Chester County Pennsylvania. Many buildings on the campus were constructed with local serpentine stone. (C)

This view of the school band has a 1908 post-mark and appears to have been taken on the steps of the Gymnasium. "The Normal Band was organized on November 22, 1889, principally to furnish march music for a military company composed of students." (C)

THE STUDENT BAND-STATE NORMAL SCHOOL, WEST CHESTER, PA.

The gymnasium was built in 1889 was the second largest gym in the nation at that time. The design by T. Roney Williamson was based upon the interior and exterior plan of the "Hemenway" gym at Harvard. (A)

Interior view of the gym during a Gymnastic exhibition. The main floor of the gymnasium is on the second floor and was 100 feet long and 60 feet wide. (C)

Basket Ball Team, State Normal School, West Chester, Pa.

The 1906-07 basketball team of the State Normal School. (C)

THE BASKET BALL TEAM - STATE NORMAL SCHOOL, WEST CHESTER, PA.

The message on the back of the card of the 1907-08 basketball team states, "This is our wonderful basketball team. Do you think you could come out sometime in February to see them play?" The postcard was sent to Doylestown, Pennsylvania. (D)

A scarce photo postcard of the school's baseball team, which appears to have been taken behind Recitation Hall on campus. (D)

Wayne Field, West Chester, Pa.   Henry's Souvenir Card.

The grandstand was built in 1900 and stood for 49 years until it was destroyed by fire. (B)

CHAPTER 14
Sharples

One of the fastest growing industries just prior to the vintage postcard era was dairy products. To accommodate the growing number of farmers who sold milk in Philadelphia, the Pennsylvania Railroad (PRR) began to install milk platforms at every station where farmers could leave special milk cans to be picked up by a train.

In 1881, Philip M. Sharples founded the Sharples Cream Separator Works to manufacture a device used to separate cream from milk. By reducing the labor needed to process milk, the cream separator enabled more people to keep a cow, and enabled farmers to specialize their product for different markets.

Sharples also utilized innovative business practices, such as advertising and multiple product lines to increase their business. After moving to a site alongside the railroad tracks on the north area of West Chester in 1889, the Sharpless Separator Works produced dairy equipment until the Great Depression.

The collecting of colorful historical advertising postcards is an active one as evidenced by the activity on Ebay online. The Sharples postcards needed to be included in this book.

Greystone Hall is at the center of a complete English country estate built in 1907 for Philip M. Sharples (1857-1944), inventor and manufacturer of the Sharples Tubular Cream Separator, which sold from the 1890's to the 1930's. A Kirby postcard. (B)

The sunken garden of the Sharples Mansion. (D)

This postcard captures the eloquence and grandeur of the estate of Greystone Hall. (A)

Greystone Hall is a Tudor Revival mansion designed by Philadelphia architect Charles Barton Keen and built in 1907 for Philip M. Sharples, the inventor and manufacturer of the Sharples Cream Separator. This great American country house is part of what was planned as a complete turn-of-the-century gentleman's country estate. Remarkably preserved, visiting Greystone Hall is a return to the age of elegance. The mansion, with exteriors of superbly pointed gray Foxcroft granite, is an architectural gem. It is an excellent example of the classic tradition in American country house architecture. A Sexichrome card. (B)

"Greystone Hall Gardens," Sharples Mansion, West Chester, Pa.

P.M. SHARPLESS MANSION BY MOONLIGHT, WEST CHESTER, Pa.

The machines, which separated the rich butterfat from raw milk, were manufactured at Sharples' factories in West Chester, Pennsylvania, and near Hamburg, Germany. After achieving worldwide financial success, Sharples began to purchase parcels of farmland just north of West Chester, ultimately assembling almost a thousand acres on which he planned to build a magnificent home and surrounding estate. A Henry postcard. (B)

After Sharples' first wife Helen died in 1911 and their three children were on their own, he remarried and with his second wife, Jean, had three more children. They lived at Greystone until 1935. His early great success was followed by financial ruin. Greystone, which had been pledged as collateral on loans, was foreclosed in the Depression and Sharples and his young family moved to Pasadena, California, where he lived until his death in 1944. A Pennsylvania Grange Convention at the estate. (D)

In 1881, Philip M. Sharples founded the Sharpless Cream Separator Works to manufacture a device used to separate cream from milk. By reducing the labor needed to process milk, the cream separator enabled more people to keep a cow, and enabled farmers to specialize their product for different markets. (C)

Herbert McCornack invented the Sharples Cream Separator, a can washer, and many other useful items. He was awarded at least 50 United States patents. A PMC card. (B)

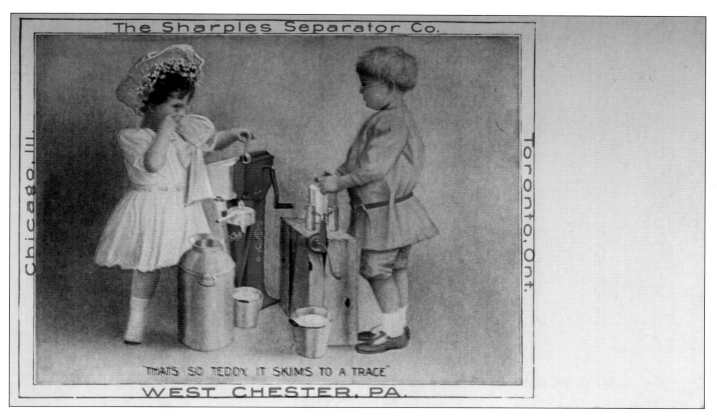

The Sharples Separator Co.

Chicago, Ill.

Toronto, Ont.

"THAT'S SO TEDDY, IT SKIMS TO A TRACE"

WEST CHESTER, PA.

Sharples Works is actually a five-acre enclave of four distinctive, historically certified brick and timber mill buildings that were built in the 1890s to house the dairy industry's first tubular cream separator. A PMC published card. (B)

The Sharples Separator Company

Chicago, Illinois

Toronto, Canada

SHARPLES TUBULAR CREAM SEPARATORS

WEST CHESTER, PA.

Sharples also utilized innovative business practices, such as advertising and multiple product lines to increase their business. After moving to a site along the railroad tracks on the north side of town in 1889, the Sharples Separator Works produced dairy equipment until the Depression, when it was acquired by the ESCO Cabinet Company. (B)

The Sharples Separator Works (1881-1933) (B)

Published by Sharples. (B)

Advertising postcards issued
by Sharples were colorful,
sometimes humorous, and
always numerous. (B)

Sharples advertising postcards were designed to be attention grabbers. (C)

The separator was first made by Gustaf de Laval in 1877. With it, it was possible to separate the cream from the milk. When it spins, the cream, which is heaviest, is pushed outward against the walls and the milk, which is lighter, is collected in the middle. Gustaf de Laval's construction made it possible to start the largest separator factory in the world, Alfa Laval AB. The milk-separator became a big advance in industry in Sweden. Within the first decade in the 1900s there were over twenty separator manufacturers in Stockholm. (Translated from the Swedish article) (B)

Sharples' wry humor.
Published by Sharples.
(C)

Preparedness on the Farm includes a Sharples Cream Separator

The Sharples Separator Company

SHARPLES TUBULAR CREAM SEPARATORS

Chicago, Illinois

Toronto, Canada

WEST CHESTER, PA.

A classic pose on this advertising postcard published by Sharples. (C)

Philip Sharples's son, Edward D. Sharples, became a dealer in cream separator supplies in Council Bluffs, Iowa. He was born in West Chester, Pennsylvania, on the March 13, 1861. In 1893 the Sharples Company opened a supply house in Council Bluffs and Edward D. Sharples then located in this city, continuing inactive connection with the business until about 1897. In 1901 he established a supply house, handling all brands of cream separators and in six months, beginning January 1, 1907, his sales amounted to forty-eight hundred separators. His business thus had a rapid and substantial growth and Mr. Sharples was well known as an enterprising merchant. (B)

When Phillip Sharples became intrigued by the cream separator, he traveled to Sweden to meet Gustav de Laval. They agreed that Sharples could manufacture DeLaval separators in the USA using certain Swedish components. In 1890 a factory to make separators was built in Poughkeepsie, New York, and this factory remained operational for separators and other Alfa Laval products until 1990. Sharples published card. (B)

THE INTRUDER!

WHO'S AFRAID?

Sharples made many improvements to the original design, and the two gentlemen ran a profitable business together from 1886 until 1892. In 1915 Sharples' son applied centrifugal technology to industrial applications and formed the Sharples Corporation. During the ensuing years, the two companies became competitors. Published by Sharples. (B)

In 1988, Sharples and Alfa Laval once again joined forces to form the largest and most advanced separation company in the world. Today, Sharples separators are a well-known part of Alfa Laval's separator product line. (A)

THE SHARPLES SEPARATOR COMPANY

WEST CHESTER, PA.

CHICAGO, ILL. TORONTO, ONT.

TUBULAR CREAM SEPARATORS

References/Bibliography

Books

Baldwin, Wm. C., & Paul A. Rodebaugh. *Chester County Postcard Album I.* Josten's, 1980

Baldwin, Wm. C., & Paul A. Rodebaugh. *Chester County Postcard Album II.* Havertown Printing, 1984

Borough of West Chester. *West Chester, The First 200 Years.* 1999.

Carson-Gentry, Martha, & Paul Rodebaugh. *Images of West Chester.* Arcadia, 1997.

Mowday, Bruce Edward. *West Chester.* Arcadia, 2005

Sturzebecker, Dr. Russell L. *Centennial History of West Chester State College.*

Internet

http://www.courses.wcupa.edu/jones/his480/riggstown.htm , 2006

http://www.dsf.chesco.org/chesco/cwp/view.asp?A, 2006

http://www.famefireco.org/history.php, 2006

http://www.freepages.books.rootsweb.com/~cooverfamily/pottawattamie_2/pot_2_24.htm

http://www.greystonehall.com/history.htm

http://www.photography.about.com/od/collectingphotos/a/a070204_3.htm , 2006

http://www.refriedjeans.com/2006

http://www.west-chester.com/harb/chapter02ptA.htm, 2006

http://www.wikipedia.org/wiki/West_Chester_Pennsylvania, 2006